SHADOW CATS

Tales from New York City's Animal Underground

Janet Jensen

Adams Media Corporation
Avon, Massachusetts

Published by
Adams Media Corporation
57 Littlefield Street, Avon, MA 02322 U.S.A.
www.adamsmedia.com

ISBN: 1-58062-752-8

Printed in Canada.

J I H G F E D C B A

Library of Congress Cataloging-in-Publication Data
Jensen, Janet
Shadow cats / Janet Jensen.
    p.   cm.
  ISBN 1-58062-752-8
  1. Feral cats—New York (State)—New York—Anecdotes. 2. Feral cats—
Behavior—New York (State)—New York—Anecdotes. 3. Urban animals—
New York (State)—New York—Anecdotes. 4. Jensen, Janet I. Title.
SF450 .J46 2002
636.8'009747'1—dc21   2002009815

This publication is designed to provide accurate and authoritative information with
regard to the subject matter covered. It is sold with the understanding that the publisher is not engaged in rendering legal, accounting, or other professional advice.
If legal advice or other expert assistance is required, the services of a competent professional person should be sought.
    —From a *Declaration of Principles* jointly adopted by a Committee of the
    American Bar Association and a Committee of Publishers and Associations

Cover photograph of cat © ImageState.
All photos courtesy of Janet Jensen, except where noted.

This book is available at quantity discounts for bulk purchases.
For information, call 1-800-872-5627.

To Casey, 1983–2002

Contents

Acknowledgments

It took considerable support to coax my first book into being. I'm grateful to everyone who helped, especially:

Daniel Berthold-Bond, for being so enthusiastic about my first piece on feral cats written for his environmental ethics class.

Gay Walley for convincing me that my cat stories were rich enough to turn into a book, and then for midwiving it into existence.

Brad Newsham, who for twenty-five years, since our days together on the *Sandpoint Daily Bee*, has been a source of inspiration and encouragement.

Mark Kuras for helping me unravel the threads of meaning the cats signified to me.

Murray, for his generosity in so many ways, and for taking such good care of Wily and Luna even though he objects to the concept of pets.

Lois, for her inflated confidence in my abilities.

Gerald, for his loving attention to me and my manuscript during its final stages. Cathy Stanton for finding me Gerald and for other contributions to my life too numerous to mention.

Julie Castiglia for finding a publisher; April Christofferson, for finding me Julie, and for decades of friendship and support.

I thank Vera and Richard and Donna and Gail and others for their unstinting commitment to animals in need, and for allowing me to write about them. I'm also very grateful to the many other rescuers and caretakers and organizations out there who are doing so much to help our feline friends.

I am also grateful to the entire team at Adams Media for their care in turning the manuscript into a book, particularly to Claire Gerus for taking a chance on it; to Paul Beatrice, Colleen Cunningham, and Daria Perreault for the striking cover and inside design; to Laura MacLaughlin for taking care of the details during the final stages of production; to Amy Collins for managing sales; and to Sophie Cathro for her assistance with publicity.

And, of course, I'm deeply indebted to the kitties, for drawing me into their lives.

Preface

No one knows how many unowned cats survive in New York City's five boroughs, but animal control officers estimate they number in the hundreds of thousands. Most of the city's street cats are feral: wary, untouchable, and, for all practical purposes, unadoptable. Obligate—and opportunistic—carnivores, these street cats eat whatever meat comes easiest: handouts, garbage scraps, rodents, insects, and when they're hungry enough and quick enough, pigeons and sparrows.

Shelter seems to be a more significant limiting factor than food. In New York, free-roaming cats take refuge in backyards, parks, cemeteries, community gardens, warehouses, scrap heaps, abandoned cars, the riprap and piers along the Hudson, railroad tunnels—even median strips. Like homeless people, some cats stay near warm spots above steam vents or seek shelter under bridges or find open basements to sleep in. Perhaps 500 make their home on Rikers Island. A year ago I came upon one family of cats curled up between the treads of a large earthmover. Street cats sometimes live on their own, but most prefer to live in family groups or tribes.

Because of the many threats to their survival, street cats race through all nine of their lives more quickly than their pampered indoor cousins. Their toughness—a cat can survive for weeks without food—means that their suffering can be quite prolonged. Perils abound. Street cats get run over or mangled by moving parts when they climb under the hoods of cars for the warmth of their engines. About half of the kittens born outdoors succumb to disease, exposure, or parasites and fleas in their first year. New York street cats are chased by vicious dogs, tormented by sadists, and even used for target practice. Those that lap up puddles of sweet-tasting but toxic antifreeze are likely to die of kidney failure.

In spite of the hazards, cat populations can quickly grow out of control. Since a female cat bears two or three litters a year, a single pair and their offspring can easily turn into a colony of thirty or forty in just two years. When their numbers become problematic and people start to complain about the yowling and spraying, street cats may be rounded up and killed by the city's Center for Animal Care and Control. Many people think there is a better way.

For more than a decade the Washington, D. C.–based group, Alley Cat Allies, has advocated dealing with free-ranging cats in a humane manner. The group recommends keeping feral cat populations under control by trapping, vetting, and neutering them, and then placing the unadoptable wild ones in managed colonies, where caretakers make sure they have food, water, and shelter. Alley Cat Allies believes these cats should not be considered pests but part of the urban wildlife community.

They assert that if their numbers are kept in check, feral cats can live reasonably long, healthy, and dignified lives, in spite of the uncertainties and the hazards. The group also believes that feral cat colonies, properly handled, actually add something to the urban fabric. Apparently some 20,000 New Yorkers who feed street cats at least occasionally think so, too. Perhaps a hundred people in New York City's five boroughs have taken on the responsibility of managing colonies of feral cats.

My early attempts to help street cats were littered with mistakes that, perhaps, others can avoid. However, since my initial efforts many resources have sprung up in New York City and in the country as a whole to guide people who want to help but aren't sure just what to do. As described in the final chapter of this book, a wide network of support is now available, catalyzed by electronic communications and, perhaps, by our evolving sense of what we owe to other sensate beings. Both Alley Cat Allies and the New York–based Neighborhood Cats have Web sites full of information and guidelines for those who want to get involved. I encourage anyone interested in the welfare of homeless cats to heed their good advice and to proceed: armed with information and with caution.

Foreword

Thousands of feral (wild) cats exist precariously in alleys, tunnels, deserted buildings, and under bridges in every major city. Others form colonies in parking lots or fields, in ditches and in woodlands, subsisting on rodents and garbage, enduring cold and snow, heat and filth until starvation, infection, accident, or attack ends their pitifully short lives. Their wretched existence breaks our hearts. Seeing them, any animal lover longs to help. "They should all be trapped and neutered," you declare to yourself, "and then good homes ought to be found for them."

"Right you are!" I agree; but three big obstacles stand in the way. First and foremost, these are wild animals we are talking about and they already have what they consider to be a very fine home—a familiar territory with a living space they have carved out for themselves with their mate and children and their own familiar circle of friends and relations who make up their colony. To a cat, familiarity breeds contentment. The last thing they want is a strange new home.

Second, wild animals are not suitable as house pets. Feral cats, almost by definition, will not allow anyone to touch them. Adjustment to life in a house or apartment can take months or even years—if they adjust at all. Such cats frequently live out their lives hiding under beds or in the back of closets. If a cat is not really a feral, but a stray with memories of living with humans in the past, or if a feral kitten begins the process of socialization when very young, sometimes patience, love, patience, and more patience can succeed.

The third, and greatest, obstacle is that we are dealing with millions of cats nationwide. There simply aren't enough homes for them. Every year, several million sweet, loving, intelligent, beautiful, healthy cats are destroyed by shelters simply because nobody wants them. Most people will look to this vast pool of ideal pets rather than try to tame a feral cat who doesn't want to be tamed in the first place. Adopting a feral is seldom the best course of action for either the cat or the prospective owner.

Tragically, rescuers who trap, neuter, and try to place feral cats in homes almost inevitably end up warehousing cats. These rescuers are trying their best, but the harsh reality that there are no homes for the cats results in the holding area or shelter becoming more and more crowded. Funds dwindle; workers become exhausted; corners must be cut on food quality, sanitation, and veterinary services. A "no kill" shelter is one whose policy is not to euthanize a healthy animal. The operative word here is "healthy." Put a wild cat into a small cage or an overcrowded room with a lot of other stressed-out cats and, if he wasn't sick when he arrived, he soon will be. Now the only question becomes: How long will each cat have to endure the purgatory of warehousing before he sickens and escapes through euthanasia? Rescuers who warehouse find themselves between a rock and a hard place. All too often it isn't just the cats that are driven to sickness or insanity by the situation.

But take heart; a solution has been found. It is called trap-neuter-return. Cats are trapped and neutered as before, but then they are returned to their home colonies. The colonies are then managed by caregivers, who can provide food, water, and sometimes, if necessary, shelters.

My own experience in this field began with Neighborhood Cats, New York City's trap-neuter-return organization. The group began by getting one colony of cats under control. Now they supervise colonies throughout the city. Recently they trapped, neutered, and released more than 180 cats living on land surrounding the city's correctional facility at Rikers Island. The organization's guiding philosophy is the first rule of medicine: first, do no harm. The trap-neuter-return approach harms neither cats nor caregivers; in fact, it benefits both. Rescuers working with this approach avoid getting burned out, and remain proud, happy, and enthusiastic.

The surrounding human communities also benefit from our managed colonies. The rodent population is controlled as before, but the neutered cats no longer fight and mate; no more yowling and spraying, and no more litters of kittens. No more puncture wounds from bites or sexual activity to spread feline leukemia and feline immunodeficiency virus. As the colony cats's health improves they become more and more beautiful and charming.

Janet Jensen's book takes us along on her own journey of compassion into the world of what she calls Shadow Cats. The human mind learns by making mistakes. Fortunately for us, Janet, like everyone else who attacked this problem, made mistakes along the way, and learned from them. But, more important, when she encountered difficulties, she didn't throw up her hands and quit; she persevered, solved the problem, and went on to run into more problems and discover more solutions. She has continued to learn, and, best of all, she generously shares her experiences with us so that we too can reap the benefits as we travel the road she took into the mysterious and fascinating world of the Shadow Cats.

Anitra Frazier,
author of *The New Natural Cat*

━ Chapter 1 ━

Encounters

Cats, no less liquid than their shadows
Offer no angles to the wind.
They slip, diminished, neat, through loopholes
Less than themselves.

—A. S. J. Tessimond, *Cats*

Walking west one morning on Delancey Street in the shadow of the approach to the Williamsburg Bridge, I noticed a rangy tabby trotting along a path between a building and an open lot, empty except for worn bricks, wilted cardboard boxes, the skeleton of a kitchen chair, a disabled shopping cart, and plastic bags flapping in the wind. The cat, taking a sharp right, ducked under an opening in the chain-link fence enclosing the area. What was he up to? I wondered. Where had he spent the night?

I regretted that I wasn't carrying, as I sometimes do, some treat that might pique a cat's interest. But the tabby, though lean, didn't appear to be starving, and he wasn't begging. He looked as if he knew the lay of the land and could take care of himself. I felt pleased that our paths should have crossed briefly as we headed on our different ways, through our vastly different realities.

At the time, like most New Yorkers, I had no idea how many cats manage to survive in this man-made landscape of concrete and brick and steel. Now I know that the city provides something of an ecological niche to tens, if not hundreds of thousands of otherwise homeless cats, who venture out late at night when most humans are asleep or who appear in response to established feedings. Like the cat I saw, the majority of these street cats are feral—the wild, untouchable progeny of domestic cats that were abandoned, lost, or, for whatever reason, had life on the streets thrust upon them.

The city's street cats came into my consciousness by degrees soon after I moved to Manhattan's Lower East Side. I had sublet a large one-bedroom co-op from Murray, my sister's partner. His brother, who had owned it originally, had died young, and Murray, wanting to keep the apartment in the family, was charging me only the co-op's low maintenance costs, a deal I couldn't afford to pass up. The flat itself was in a quiet, seven-story complex surrounding a grassy courtyard, complete with fountain and reflecting pool.

The nearby neighborhood spreads out south from Houston Street and east of the subway lines, where the regular grid of Manhattan gives way to a skewed scrabble of tilted streets, short alleys, and deserted cul-de-sacs. It's one of the few parts of the city where vacant lots have not yet all been built on, abandoned buildings are not all cleaned up, and basement windows are not all sealed shut. These are features that make it habitable for cats.

The first sign of cats was the empty cat food tins I noticed near the back entrance of my building. I asked Murray, who had played in the courtyard as a child, about them. "There have always been cats around here," he said. "People have always fed them." So, for a time, I just accepted their mostly invisible presence. But when I asked the maintenance man about them, he said he had come across fifteen skeletons in the basement. That's when I started to get concerned.

Photo courtesy of Meredith Weiss

Since then I've gotten to know all the cats on my block: their shifting allegiances, their family histories, their distinctive traits, personalities, and habits. I've spent countless hours waiting for cats to get hungry enough to walk into traps and then carting them to those vets who are willing to deal with wild animals. Over the years I have found myself, from time to time, slinking into dark and creaky boiler rooms in search of kittens, and lowering myself through broken windows. After dark I tend to lower my gaze and stay attuned to movement in the shadows. Gradually I've become someone whose nostrils widen at a whiff of cat spray, more out of curiosity than distaste. Who has been by? I wonder. How long ago?

Over the same period I have come to know a wide circle of quirky, devoted, and, for the most part, wonderful people, members of what the *New York Times* called "the animal underground," and what Cleveland Amory termed "the army of the kind": Donna, the stalwart champion of animals; Richard, a songwriter and musician when he isn't out trapping; Gail, the psychic animal communicator; Vera, the kindhearted Berliner who over the years rescued hundreds of kittens; and a whole network of other people looking out for street cats in different ways.

When my stance toward the cats changed from mild interest to concern, I began focusing on a group of five or six that I'd sometimes find hanging around near the back entrance of the courtyard after dark. Their hanging around, I learned, meant the regular feeders hadn't shown up. Back then the cats were simply a little band of outsiders with a shifting cast I enjoyed seeing from time to time. It was when I got to know them as individuals—gimpy Nicholas, magnificent Aloysius, soulful Mimi and her brood, slinky Tammy—that they became impossible for me to ignore.

The outdoor cats started to occupy more of my attention when a litter of four kittens appeared one day in early winter in a corner of the interior courtyard. Because of the way my building is shaped, with alcoves and recesses, some parts of the courtyard are wider than others. The mother cat had made her home in a far corner of one of the wide stretches a few yards from the sidewalk, near the door to an empty storage area. Even when the door was shut, there was enough clearance that the cats could scoot under it. A couple of open vents nearby offered alternative escape routes, so it seemed the mother cat had picked a fairly safe spot.

Besides shelter and safety, her choice of location offered another advantage as well: it was directly below the apartment of a woman who lowered a tin of cat food suspended from a string through her window a couple of times a day. Since the mother cat was now living around the corner from the rest of the tribe in the park, she and her kittens got first dibs at the food. When cat lovers in the complex realized there was a litter of kittens in the courtyard, the daily rations increased. I started being less casual about my contributions and made it a point every day to bring a little something for the brood. I began to feel that the kittens depended on me. They were along my path to work every morning, too adorable to simply pass by. They always seemed hungry. As the days passed, their appetites, as well as their expectations, grew quickly. I started bringing food in the morning, and I'd stop to pick up a can or two of cat food before I came through the courtyard again at night. When I called, "Here kitty, kitty," four little furry critters would run toward me. Soon, before I'd even called out, they were able to recognize me from halfway across the courtyard.

"Don't you just love the way they gallop toward you when they see you coming?" asked one of the other feeders.

Of course I did. I was hooked. It is very seductive to be known and appreciated by wild animals.

The babies included two tabbies, a blue-gray beauty, and one tuxedo, who was the smallest and shiest of the litter. But one snowy night when I came by with food, the family was gone except for the shy one, the little black and white. And he looked terrible.

His nose was runny, his eyes were caked, and he wheezed. He seemed to have been deserted by his family. I brought him chicken broth or soft food a couple of times a day. I tried to coax him out and to get close enough so I could scruff him up and take him to the vet. I thought I should rescue the kitten but had no idea how to go about doing so. I called a few agencies with little success. One offered to rent me a trap for $100, but the office was way uptown. I was going crazy at work and couldn't figure a way to pick it up during business hours. The sick kitten seemed to want to come closer, but fear overruled his instinct to come for help. Each day his nasal congestion got thicker, his eyes more caked, his meows more plaintive. And then one morning he didn't come out at all. For two years the image of that sick kitten dying alone in the cold, wet, dark space under my building pricked my conscience. The desire to avoid feeling so helpless and guilty again was what initiated the series of events described in this book. 🐾

~ Chapter 2 ~

Impractical Cats

Being with wild animals—whether they're squirrels in the backyard, or heavily antlered elk in Yellowstone—reminds us of our own wildness, thrills the animal part of us that loves the feel of sunlight and the succulence of fresh water, is alert to danger and soothed by the familiar sound of family and herd.

—*Diane Ackerman,* Deep Play

After the tuxedo kitten died, the courtyard looked and felt empty. I went back to minding my own business. I stayed away from the little park next door unless I happened to have leftover meat that I didn't want to throw in the garbage. Occasionally I'd catch sight of a cat or two slinking down the back alley or dashing through the park.

Nevertheless, a few months later I found myself, steel bar in hand, trying to tamper inconspicuously with a vent opening so that a new litter of kittens would not be entombed in the basement. And soon thereafter, wild cats were crouching in my bathroom, scampering through my dreams, and taking me on a journey that has gone on for about five years now, and to which I see no end in sight.

It all started one balmy evening just before I was to take off for a summer session of graduate school upstate. Passing through the courtyard, I noticed the big, fluffy, marmalade tom that the security guards called Garfield copulating with a lean tabby. Intercourse is a quick, frenzied matter between cats: some exploratory nuzzles, then frantic skirmishing as the male mounts his mate, followed by the female's scream as he removes his barbed penis (they "mate as fiercely as they kill" writes Vita Sackville-West). It all takes just a few minutes. The naturalist in me felt privileged to have caught the action.

Two months later when I returned home, I noticed the same two cats—Garfield and Mimi—loping toward the back entrance of the courtyard. I was alarmed to find them both painfully skinny, looking like no more than bags of skin and fur. "Here kitty, kitty, kitty," I called in the high-pitched voice to which all cats seem to respond. The two stopped dead in their tracks— perhaps they recognized the voice of a feeder. "Stay here," I said, trying hard to communicate on a level that would be understood without words. "I'll be right back with some food." I rushed inside, took the lumbering elevator up seven floors, grabbed a can of cat food from my kitchen stash, ran down the stairs, and went outside. Whether the cats had intuited my message or remembered me as a food source, they had decided to wait around.

The pair ate in hurried gulps and then ran off, seeming pleased with dinner but evidently caring not a whit about my company. The following day one of the maintenance men pointed out the new courtyard litter of kittens. No wonder Mimi was so skinny—she must have been depleted from the burden of bearing and nursing kittens. And toms, I learned, sometimes also try to help feed the youngsters.

Once again the anticipation of seeing the kittens and watching their antics enlivened my passage through the courtyard each morning. When they heard my call or the metallic snap of a tin of food popping open, their heads would bob up from their hole in the wall. At first, huddled together and moving with flexible, seemingly jointless limbs, they looked like liquid fur, spilling down in unison from the open vent and then shape-shifting into four furry mounds. Later, emboldened, they'd bound out separately from different openings, each now bearing a distinctive demeanor and personality. The tiny tabby with the almond-shaped eyes and a face marked like a heart, Wily, was always the last to get to the food and the first to dart off when I took a step in her direction. The larger, darker tabby, Scamper, was the first to greet me and was almost brave enough to eat from my hand. The remaining two littermates were almost identical blue-grays; one, Bandit, was distinguished by one cloudy eye that gave him a cockeyed, soulful look. Since he was shier than his brother, I wondered if the scuffle that had injured his eye had left him cautious of life. No matter how the kittens positioned themselves at mealtimes, they took great care to maintain a clear path to at least one of their vents so they could scramble to safety when scared. When they were deeply engaged in eating, I'd sometimes try to edge closer. But when I reached a certain point, as if an alarm had sounded, they'd scatter like billiard balls and leap for the safety of various openings in the wall.

Mimi was a dutiful mother, alert and watchful. She always let the little kittens eat before she did. Occasionally, with a bit of a swagger, Garfield would shoulder them aside and commandeer a place at the food. I had rarely seen him during the day until the kittens were born, but afterward, when they were all playing together, he often perched near the group, sitting nobly and, to my mind, proudly on a slight rise in the grass, soaking up the sun.

The kittens' food consumption increased daily and they were growing quickly. What had started out as an offering of a small can or two of food each day became, within a couple of months, a ten-pound bag of kitten chow per week, along with some canned food and leftovers. I tried to pick up afterward and throw away the paper plates and tinfoil other feeders had left. Despite my efforts, though, the corner was frequently a bit of a mess. The usually congenial maintenance man started to complain. "Myself," he said, "I love cats. I have one of my own at home. But the management doesn't want them here. People are complaining."

Suddenly the openings that the kittens had been using to come and go became unreliable. The metal door and the vent covers that gave the cats access to the courtyard were being closed and latched at night. Whenever I passed by, I would open the latch, and I noticed that others were doing the same. All day long, the maintenance men would shut the door; all day long, passing cat lovers would reopen it. When the doors began to be closed more often than they were open, I started to panic. The cats, I thought, must be getting confused and scared as the rules kept changing.

One evening—by this time we were well into winter and the weather had turned cold—I looked around and realized that this litter of darling kittens had become a tribe of four fairly good-sized cats plus Mimi and Garfield. Furthermore, the two females would soon be coming into heat. All those bags of cat food I had brought down had been transformed into flesh and blood and muscle, all four kittens were now big, healthy teenagers, and it seemed they were my problem as much as anyone's. The tribe's increased activity and presence were attracting attention, both feline and human. Other cats from the nearby park started coming by to socialize or to eat; the large bush the kittens had once used as a fortress began to smell strongly of cat spray. People emerging from the nearby entry told me that their lobby reeked. For some reason, all the time I was blithely feeding the little kittens, I hadn't looked ahead to this point. But now it was painfully clear that the courtyard was too small for so many cats and for any new kittens that might be born.

The situation was growing more complicated because of the changing financial structure of the co-op, which had been built in the early 1930s as a kind of communal enterprise. Originally one could become a "co-operator" for just $24 a room with full owner's rights, except that the unit couldn't be sold for a profit. But the cooperative would soon be "going private," as had similar complexes nearby. The possibility of large sums of money sloshing around naturally changed things. The co-op board had hired a go-getting new manager, and plans were being laid to re-landscape the courtyard, paint the foyers, and install bigger brass mailboxes and new elevators. A tribe of stray cats, with their smells, caterwauling, messes, and fleas, was not part of the plan.

I knew I had to do something, but I wasn't sure what. "Call Donna Mitchell," my sister Lois advised, reminding me how invaluable her assistance had been a couple of years earlier, after

Lois had taken pity on a howling and shaking old dog she had come across near Central Park. Pippin was initially taken by police to the Center for Animal Care and Control, where he would almost certainly have been killed. Even though he was too old and traumatized to be adoptable, Donna was able to spring him from CACC and talk Lois through all the available options. Though she was trying to extricate herself from the rescue business, which had left her physically and financially drained, Donna had spent hours on the phone patiently coaching Lois, networking, and trying to find foster homes or sheltered situations that might be right for Pippin. She finally identified an animal sanctuary that would foster him indefinitely for a substantial financial contribution, which she offered to help with. Lois had been tremendously impressed by her mettle.

When I reached Donna and started to describe what was going on, she was ready to help. She immediately grasped the urgency of the situation and provided the clarity and experience I lacked. "There's not a minute to lose," she said. "The management's cracking down, the cats are losing their shelter, the snow's going to fly. We have to get those cats out of there. I'll make some calls and get back to you before the weekend." Presidents' Day was coming up, and the three-day weekend seemed like a good time to get started. I was busy on Friday night, I told Donna, but I'd make myself available over the rest of the weekend.

But no one called.

The next day, as he picked up a bowl of uneaten cat food near the cats' corner nook, the maintenance man advised me that feeding was no longer allowed. "The management wants the cats out of here," he said. "They're holding us responsible if they find plates and cat food around." I explained that a rescue operation was imminent. "That's good," he said, "because they can't stay here."

Three of the four access points from the crawl space to the courtyard were now routinely kept closed. The cats had moved their base of operations to the fourth vent, which was fitted with a slatted valance to let air in and out. If the valance had been new and properly fitted, the cats couldn't have passed through it at all. But it was bent a bit and loose on its casing, so the cats could squeeze in and out between the brick wall and the loose metal frame. Each time they entered the courtyard, the frame clattered loudly against the wall. For creatures whose well-being depends, to a certain extent, on their ability to move about silently, the noise must have been terribly unnerving.

That weekend I started feeding the cats near this new point of entry. One evening at dusk my sister accompanied me. "There's a tiny gray kitten there, too," she pointed out. Though I didn't see it, she assured me that there was a gray kitty much smaller than the others. I couldn't figure out where it had come from: To my knowledge, Mimi hadn't been pregnant again, and Wily was still too young to have given birth. Later I surmised that Mimi had adopted the gray foundling and his sister.

I was growing increasingly anxious. I knew the valance would eventually be tightened, and now there was at least one new kitten to worry about—and possible littermates. The weekend passed, and I'd still had no word from Donna or the rescuers, whose phone numbers were not readily given out, especially to someone so new to the business.

Sunday night I left a message to let Donna know I hadn't heard from anyone. Monday I heard nothing; Tuesday no word. That evening when I came home, I found the last vent sealed. The steel frame was glued to the brick wall with a waxy substance. Scamper, the brave tabby, was sniffing at the closed vent and meowing to his fellow tribe members locked inside. The poignancy and injustice of Scamper trying to reunite with his family in a world suddenly changed by human intervention was more than I could bear. Out by the alley I found a steel lever, which I used to pry loose and remove three of the metal bars in the valance so the cats could get in and out.

After removing the slats in the valance, I went upstairs and lay down, drained by anxiety about what might happen next. Undoubtedly my monkey wrenching was only a temporary measure; surely the building managers would not leave the vent open for long. I called Donna and left yet another message, this one describing how urgent the situation had become. But she didn't call back. The next morning on my way to work, I tried to bargain with the maintenance man: Leave the vents open for just a couple more days, and I'll get the cats out of there. "We'd like to," he told me, "but you have to talk to the management. They don't want the cats around. People have been complaining."

He also claimed that the cats weren't actually locked up—he said the crawl space connected inside to an underground tunnel network, and that there were other ways to get outdoors. But when I went around to the other side of the building where the exit was supposed to be, I saw no cat-ways. Nor had I ever seen any cats at the alleged exit on that far side of the building.

Photo courtesy of Meredith Weiss

And when I looked through the valance in the courtyard, a couple pairs of gleaming eyes reflected back at me. As far as I could tell, the cats had been entombed.

Calling from my office, I left another message for Donna. When she returned the call later that afternoon, her voice was feeble and apologetic. She was terribly sorry, she said, but she had been in the hospital on intravenous antibiotics for four days, with a fever that had reached 105 degrees. "I'm feeling better now," she said weakly. "I'll get right back on the case."

"What's wrong?" I asked.

"My cat bit me," she said, with no trace of anger or sarcasm in her voice.

"Does this happen often?"

"Every once in awhile he takes a little nip," she answered. Donna's old cat Louie, a tom she had rescued years ago, had sunk his teeth deeply into her hand. I had never heard of anyone getting bitten by a cat so badly as to require hospitalization. But I learned that when a cat bite penetrates deeply, especially into a joint or tendon, it often results in a serious internal infection. Donna had cleaned the wound carefully, but by the next day she had such a high fever she had to bow out of her scheduled appearance as Gertrude in an off-Broadway production of Hamlet and take herself to the emergency room instead.

When I described the latest courtyard developments, she promised to make a few calls and see if she could get someone to trap the cats the next night.

In the meantime, I wrote letters to both the building manager and the maintenance supervisor explaining the trapping and rescue operation that we planned, taking care to acknowledge that the cats would be relocated. Because I wanted to suggest that a whole organization of animal advocates was behind the rescue, I put the letter on stationery from City Critters, the grassroots group with which Donna was loosely affiliated.

After I was sure the supervisor would have had a chance to read the letter, I called and explained the planned rescue.

"That's good," he said. "We want them out of there."

"But we need the vents left open for another few days so we can catch them," I said. It seemed like a reasonable request.

"We're not leaving the vents open." His voice suddenly went sharp and testy. "If the cats die down there, it's too bad." When I reached the building manager, she told me pretty much the same thing.

On returning home that evening, I saw that the valance I had pried open the night before had been replaced with a thick steel plate. The other doors were now secured with padlocks. Looking from the padlocks to the solid metal plate, I felt sad and defeated: I had waited too long. My chance at rescuing the family had failed by just a few days. I'd failed to rescue the little tuxedo kitten so long ago, and now I was losing these cats as well. All the exhilaration I had felt when Donna first told me that the rescue was on turned into its reverse. I felt devastated and powerless.

But imagining the cats' trauma and their probable entomb-ment, I couldn't simply give up. "There has to be a solution," I told myself with as much conviction as I could muster. And taking a deep breath, I affirmed to myself, to the universe, and to whomever else might be listening: "There is a perfect solu-tion." I considered trying to find the other end of the tunnel I had been told about and luring the cats through it with tuna, but the idea of crawling into the dark, deserted, cobweb-filled underbelly of the building seemed distasteful and a touch out-landish. Then I noticed that the steel plate closing off the cats' doorway was held to its frame by just five screws. I would wait for the courtyard to empty, so that I could try unscrewing the plate. Even if I couldn't liberate the cats, perhaps I could at least get some food to them.

Screwdriver in hand, I quietly managed to remove four of the five screws. Although I couldn't loosen the fifth one and was starting to ruin the screw, I discovered I could rotate the steel plate around it. The trickiest part of the operation was to avoid attracting attention.

The courtyard was quiet on this raw winter night. Eight different lobbies opened onto the courtyard, each one leading to thirty-five apartments, most of which housed an older crowd—some of the residents had been there since the building opened in 1931—who didn't often go out at night. I decided to try to get the support of the security guard, a gentle-faced Caribbean fellow with whom I had exchanged occasional nods. When I told him what I was doing in the shadows behind the bushes, he proved sympathetic. He had, after all, gotten to know the cats as well as anyone. Night after night, they were his entertainment. He had watched them race across the courtyard by the light of the moon, making up for their daytime reticence. He had witnessed the nightly parade of tomcats coming through the courtyard to take turns spraying one particular bush. He had noted the nightly antics of the youngsters, the fighting, and the couplings. With him on my side, I felt more at ease.

A couple of people strolled by while I was in the bushes, but even if they noticed my activities, no one said anything. When the plate swung around, I called in my high cat voice, "Here kitty, kitty," but though I saw a couple pairs of eyes peering out at me, nobody came out. "It's just me," I said. "You know me." I couldn't blame them if they didn't trust anyone anymore. Since the night was cold, I told the security guard I was going to leave the vent open for an hour or two. I left some food and came back to close it up a few hours later, so the morning crew wouldn't suspect anything.

"Tomorrow night," Donna said. I was to pick up Richard the trapper around eight. First I needed to get some fishy-smelling cat food—tuna or sardines—and figure out a place where the trapped cats could stay overnight. I had the idea that the cats would be trapped and removed, and the problem would be solved in a day or two. But in fact I had only the vaguest notion of what I was really getting into and where it would lead. 🐾

— Chapter 3 —

The Rescue

The respect principle, as a principle of justice, requires more than that we not harm some . . . [i]t also imposes the *prima facie* duty to assist those who are the victims of injustice at the hands of others.

—*Tom Regan,* The Case for Animal Rights

The following evening I left my apartment, armed once again with a screwdriver, to open the cats' vent before picking up Richard, who lived in the East Village about a mile from my place. When I arrived at the address Donna had given me, a slender, somewhat frail-looking guy with a mop of curly black hair was standing at the curb, two wire mesh traps and a cat carrier at his feet. Before we set off, he carefully ticked off everything we'd need: I had the food, the screwdriver, and a towel; he had traps, paper plates, and big, thick, leather gloves from the hardware store. We were ready to get started.

It was a bit difficult making conversation with Richard at first because he usually wears earplugs to protect his sensitive eardrums, damaged, he said, "from twenty years of rock and roll." But when he heard about the cats' situation and the indifference of the building managers, he was aghast. "Don't they understand that we're trying to save lives?" he asked in disbelief. It was clear to me that they didn't, that they were operating under a different set of moral assumptions. To the building management, the cats were the equivalent of vermin: expendable pests whose well-being was unimportant, especially when measured against human concerns. To Richard and Donna, these were unique, intelligent "subjects of a life," as animal rights philosopher Tom Regan puts it, creatures that should be rescued and cared for, especially since they were in their precarious situation because of human actions.

The cats were out and hungry when we arrived. Richard worked gracefully and methodically, setting out the metal traps. He placed tuna at the far end and dribbled what he called a *lead*, a trail of bits of food and juice, from the bait to the entrance of the trap. Usually cats have to be quite hungry to enter the wire traps; they seem instinctively wary of entering these boxy enclosures, about two and a half feet long and a foot square at either end. One end is hinged to open into the cage and hooks lightly to the top. When a cat tries to grab the bait, it steps on a plate toward the far end, the catch releases, and the door snaps shut.

We put the trap on the spot where I had been leaving food. When I called the cats, they came running—as they always had before and never would again.

First we caught the little gray kitten, and then Mimi.

When the trapdoor swung down on her and she struggled, frenzied, against the trap, the big red tom, Garfield, her consort, came over, as if to see what he could do. As powerful as he was in the cat world, he was helpless in this situation. Mimi had been pulled out of his life by forces beyond his control. As she fought against the cage, a few yards away I saw a kitten I hadn't seen before, a little tortoiseshell, leaping high into the air, twisting, turning, dancing in the moonlight, as if to exorcise her fear.

The moon was full that first night we trapped, and I had never seen so much activity in the courtyard. As soon as we got set up with the food in the traps and the cats starting to sniff at it, a group of people came through the courtyard, wanting to hang out and watch or simply to find out what was going on. One guy, a garrulous, drunken redhead with a somewhat scary smile, was the most problematic. It seemed that some of the older cat lovers in the building were watching the action from behind their curtains, and they thought we were up to no good. This man had appointed himself to represent their interests.

"Look, I know the people who run this neighborhood, and we don't want you trapping the cats," he said, with a menacing grin. He talked on nonstop, dropping the names of local politicians, suggesting that we were taking the cats to Chinese restaurants, and mentioning a powerful bouncer thug he knew. "This guy's so big and brawny, you'd never suspect he was infected with HIV," he said.

"The old people around here want the cats left alone," he continued, and then he insisted that he be given one of the cats for his girlfriend. "We love animals," he said, but he wouldn't believe that we did, too. He peeled off two hundred-dollar bills from a roll of cash and tried to offer them in return for a cat. Thinking of all the vet bills we would be mounting up, I considered taking the money. But Richard, a musician who struggled to make ends meet, wouldn't consider it.

Over and over, we tried to explain why we were trapping the cats. We couldn't seem to make the self-appointed watchdog understand that they were in danger and that we were trying to help. "I don't want you trapping anymore tonight," he said in a threatening tone. "Not until I check you people out."

Richard was nervous. "What is *he* doing to help these animals?" he asked. And he wondered aloud if the guy might have a gun.

I was more worried about local politics, and paranoid, as usual, about the possibility of losing my sublet. In any case, we stopped trapping for the night.

The guy—his name was Dave, I found out—acted as if he owned the neighborhood. So when I ran into him a couple of mornings later, sober and walking his dog, I thought I'd see whether his connections could buy us some time. By then he was more amiable. He had "checked us out" by calling the veterinarian where I had taken the cats.

"Since you know the people who run things around here, maybe you could get them to leave the vents open for a few more days," I suggested. "That would really help us get the cats out of there."

"The most I can buy you is a day," he replied with a straight face, apparently forgetting all the powerful connections he had claimed just a few nights before.

When the metal door snaps shut on a trap, a feral cat reacts violently, throwing itself at the sides of the cage with tremendous muscular force, flapping back and forth within the enclosure like a bass in a net, twisting and turning with the amazing spinal flexibility that allows it to maneuver within the small enclosure. To keep the cat from injuring itself, a trapper should be nearby, ready to wrap a towel around the cage and let the darkness and the sense of boundaries calm the cat down.

Transferring a cat from cage to carrier is serious business, as well. Before we transferred Mimi, Richard looked disapprovingly around my bathroom, testing the latch and screen on my seventh-floor window. "Better get anything made of glass out of here," he said, looking at the little bottles on my shelf. "It can get pretty wild if she escapes."

Later, when a kitten escaped during the transfer, I got a vivid demonstration of the possible origin of the expressions "letting the cat out of the bag" and "bouncing off the walls." A wild cat unleashed indoors practically flies across the room, first heading for a window or mirror or anything that looks like a potential escape route. Failing to exit, the cat leaps from one slight protrusion to another, dangling from moldings and window frames and towel racks. Almost in defiance of gravity, it can propel itself up walls, spring across rooms, and do pretty much anything this side of hanging from the ceiling.

During each transfer from trap to carrier, I stood behind the carrier to keep it from moving backward. Richard, with his thick gloves, opened the door of the trap into the carrier, tilting it to get the cat moving forward. The critical movement was to swing the carrier door shut before the cat realized what was happening and bolted out into the room. My earlier visions of letting the kitties loose in the bathroom, of, perhaps, petting them, were clearly flawed: These were wild animals, nothing like any of the cats I had previously known and loved.

After we'd caught and managed to transfer Mimi, the gray kitten, and the third cat, Wily, into the carrier, Richard asked, "So what are you going to do with them?"

"I don't know," I said. "I thought you would know." Donna hadn't coached me on next steps.

"I just trap," he said, sounding agitated. "Usually there's a plan. There's no plan in place here. This is no good. What are we going to do with these cats?"

What indeed? I wondered. I had thought it was all arranged. I had thought the rescuers came and handled these things. But, as I now grasped, it's not that easy. There are simply too many animal emergencies happening all the time in the city, and the rescuers, who are all volunteers, quickly get burned out. It is possible to find people willing to coach and guide you and to provide advice and phone numbers. But if you do manage to trap a feral cat, you get to deal with the consequences. Feral cats are not readily adoptable. No-kill shelters typically take only friendly, healthy cats, and then only if they have room. There simply aren't many options for placing feral cats, which is why I now try to release them back into their own familiar territory unless their situation has changed.

I was starting to get anxious about what would happen in the morning. I had recently started a lucrative freelance copy-writing job at an ad agency and had a 10:00 A.M. meeting. But I certainly couldn't leave the cats in carriers in the bathroom longer than overnight—they would need to eat, drink, excrete. And since I had to keep the door closed to keep my own cat away from fleas or any diseases the outdoor cats might be carrying, the bathroom, even with the window open, heated up like a sauna from the hot water riser. In any case, no veterinarians were available until morning. Richard gave me the names of two doctors that might take them, if I got in a jam.

I woke up early and called Donna, waking her up. I had to get moving by nine at the latest, and I had two loads of cats to take down to my car. I had to find out where I was going and figure out someplace to leave the car for the day. "The first thing is, don't panic," Donna said when I reached her, in her calm, clear, strong voice.

How can I possibly stay calm? I wondered. I have three terrified animals caged in my bathroom and no idea what to do with them.

After a few more phone calls, we worked it out. Dr. Cotter, formerly with the Humane Society, now had his own practice and was

working with City Critters. I was to bring in a check for $200, and United Action for Animals, a funding organization, would pay the rest of the vet bill for the entire tribe, including neutering, shots, flea and parasite treatment, and feline immunodeficiency virus (FIV) and feline leukemia tests. They would pay to board the cats for one week, as well. City Critters would take any young kittens. The rest was up to me.

I let my supervisor at work know that I might be a little late, loaded up the cats, and tried to drive smoothly up FDR

Drive to 65th Street, so as not to frighten my captives unnec-
essarily. They were silent, as feral cats usually are. In wild
communities, feral cats primarily communicate by using a
repertoire of visual and olfactory cues. Domestic cats develop a
language of meows because they quickly realize that humans
are not well attuned to their other forms of communication.
"Housecats," writes Roger Tabor in *The Wild Life of the
Domestic Cat*, "note that our world is largely triggered by sound
signals and so to make clear their meaning, and to prevent being
overlooked, they increase the use of their voice." For the feral
cats I took in, silence seemed to be an extension of their incli-
nation to remain invisible. The only sounds my feral cats ever
made were terribly plaintive cries in situations of abject
terror—like the time I was carrying the little gray kitten across
a noisy intersection—or cries of distress when left alone in the
bathroom for the first time.

Richard couldn't help me trap the next night, but my sister
came by and kept me company as we stood out in the damp
cold. After our initial success—three catches on the first night—
the trapping got progressively harder. The cats now knew to
distrust the wire contraption. "You go in and you don't come
out," must have been the received wisdom.

A night or two later Richard helped again, and we got two
more, Bandit and Scamper. Bandit was the blue-gray kitty with
one cloudy eye. Scamper, his brave littermate, almost escaped
in my bathroom as we moved him from cage to carrier. With
sheer force, Richard pushed back the little head that was trying

so hard to force open the carrier door. Like the rest of the family, Scamper was "spring-loaded," as Natasha, the vet's wife and colleague, described them. They all had to be sedated for their examination. But, protected with her big, thick gloves, stalwart Natasha managed to handle the cats every day. None was aggressive, she said, but Scamper was the only one who didn't seriously object to the handling, and after a few days he seemed to enjoy it.

By the time we trapped Scamper and Bandit, sweet Wily, the soft, fawn-colored tabby, whose wide green eyes looked as if they were rimmed with thin black eyeliner, was living in my bathroom. Her week with Dr. Cotter had expired, and I had nowhere else to put her. At that time, I naively thought I could get her to come around in a matter of a few weeks. She was, after all, still young. But I had no concept then of the glacial pace at which a feral cat's fear subsides, if, indeed, it ever does.

For the first couple of days, Wily generally stayed crouched in the back of the carrier I had left between the toilet and the bathtub: her new little home. At night I'd occasionally hear things falling off the windowsill and the shelf above the sink, as Wily explored all the surfaces and ledges in the small room. The bathroom was the only room I could close off, and though it seemed really tiny, Natasha and Donna assured me that the smaller the space it occupied, the safer a feral cat would feel.

I was glad Wily moved around at night; I wanted her to have that semblance of freedom. The few times I heard little *meows* coming from the room in the middle of the night, I ran in to offer soft words, even though I wasn't sure my presence was much of a comfort. Or I'd bring her a tidbit to eat, even though she never ate in my presence.

In responding to her squeaky cries, I was trying to encourage her vocalization and to foster communication, thinking it might assuage her sense of isolation. I wanted her to know that she was being heard. Beyond that, I was touched by her plaintive wail and captivated by her beautiful, heart-shaped face. Poor Wily. It seemed unfair that she, always so timid, so reluctant to get into dangerous situations, was one of the first to get caught.

With two big meals of premium kitten food every day and assorted snacks, little Wily was getting noticeably bigger. She was starting to look uncomfortably large for her small carrying-case home. The one time I tried to touch her, when she was trying to hide in a cardboard box I had placed in the bathtub, she went ballistic, springing to the towel rack, leaping and clinging to the top of the shower curtain, and then lunging toward the shelf where I kept my cosmetics and potions. In none of those places could she get a firm footing, so she ended up hanging from her front paws. Like Wile E. Coyote, the car-toon character, she got into one position and then another, moving too fast to be seen in between. "It's okay, it's okay, it's okay," I said in a low voice, turning off the light and fleeing the room so that she would calm down.

Once the rescue operation began and for months afterward, it seemed like all my free time was spent dealing with cats. Every night, as long as some of the cats were still locked up under the building, I'd go down and unscrew the vent, and if I didn't have time to trap, I'd at least put food on the ledge and give the cats a chance to come outside. Sometimes Richard would help me; sometimes other friends came by. Mostly we watched as the remaining two cats, the tortoiseshell kitten and her gray older brother, danced around the trap, refusing to go in.

In addition to my courtyard activities, I'd try to spend at least half an hour in the bathroom every day, talking softly to Wily and to Mimi, who had now come back from the vet's office and joined her daughter. I was trying to ease the haunted look in their eyes and watched for any sign of a letdown in their hunched, guarded postures. I also had to make frequent expeditions for cat food and litter, and numerous trips to the vet's uptown: bring cats in, pick them up a few days later, return them in six weeks for booster shots. I had to drop off stool samples, pick up worming medications, and when I thought my apartment was infested with fleas, a topical flea treatment. It was never absolutely clear that I did, in fact, have a flea problem, or whether I had what Natasha called "psychological fleas." Dr. Cotter hadn't seen any telltale flea dirt on the cats. But a few days after the feral cats came into the house, my own cat, Casey, started scratching and went at her ear so hard she drew blood. I started feeling little bites myself, even though I never saw any fleas. Were they actual bites, I kept wondering, or just random sensations that I ordinarily wouldn't notice? I'm still not sure.

In my downtime at the office, I put signs around and networked. I called anyone who knew anyone else who might want a cat, and then called anyone they suggested. It was soon clear that most people who wanted cats already had them. I was surprised at the number of people I discovered who already had six, eight, ten, or a dozen cats and no room for one more. And almost anyone who wanted a cat wanted a sweet, cuddly one, not a wild, unpredictable animal that might hide under a couch or behind a stove for months, offering almost nothing in the way of the positive reinforcement one seeks from a pet.

Throughout the rescue operation I was in almost daily contact with Donna, my coach and cheerleader. She never tired of hearing every detail about the cats, and she never seemed to forget a thing. She told me what to expect from feral cats, recommended people for me to call, and encouraged me when I felt overwhelmed. With Mimi and Wily in my apartment and other cats piling up at the vet's, I began to wonder why I was working so hard to trap the last two cats. "Just keep it up," Donna kept saying. "You're doing brilliantly." She did more than coach. One day she came by to check out the situation and help me trap. She also screened prospective cat owners, and eventually fostered the last two little kittens.

With Donna egging me on, I finally caught the last two. One was the tortoiseshell kitten I had seen dancing in the moonlight that night; she was usually so elusive I had glimpsed her only occasionally. With her dark brown and black markings, she was hard to see in the shadows. But the few times I did see her little face peering out of the vent, it was a striking visage: the light brown shadings on her face were in the same place as those of a chimpanzee. In the dark the other colors receded, and I felt as if I were looking at the face of a tiny simian.

One night this kitten was poised within the trap, but she carefully avoided stepping on the plate that would spring the door. At just the right moment, however, someone slammed the nearby lobby door. Startled by the noise, the kitten jumped forward, hit the plate, and was ours.

That left the last gray male, Bear, all alone for weeks. When I was too busy to trap, I pushed plates of food through the vent; it was always completely gone by the next day. I kept thinking about how lonely and frightened Bear must be. Finally I stopped feeding him for a couple of days, and hunger forced him to enter a trap for the tuna fish within. Before going in, he let out two long, sad wails that seemed to express the agony of having to decide between two unacceptable choices: starvation and entrapment.

And then there were no more cats under the building. Garfield still sauntered through nightly to spray his favorite bush, but his courtyard must have seemed very empty. 🐾

— Chapter 4 —

Talking
to Cats

But ask now the beasts, and they shall
teach thee.

—Job 12:7

Photo courtesy of Meredith Weiss

Everyone who lived in my apartment complex knew the big red tom that the security guards called Garfield. Although urban cats mainly roam late at night and in the early morning hours while most humans are asleep, Garfield showed up in the daytime quite often when the kittens were little, like a good daddy. One of the local stores gave him regular handouts. The maintenance men and security guards admired his lordly presence, his swagger, and his apparent freedom to come and go. He was wizened, battle-scarred, and mangy, but a king nonetheless.

No disrespect was meant, I think, and none taken, by naming him Garfield after the comic strip cat. But Garfield was not his real name.

I found out his real name from him, through Gail DeSciose. Gail, a former elementary school teacher, was a secret ally in my animal escapades—she was my direct communication channel with the animal world. Even Donna, I believe, was impressed by my marshaling of this particular resource. Despite all her years of experience with strays, rescues, housecats, animal organizations, adoption outlets, animal fanatics, cat colonies, veterinarians, and public relations, with all her resources across the city and beyond, Donna had never taken advantage of the services of an animal communicator.

Eyebrows raise slightly, and those less polite roll their eyes, when I mention the animal communicator. Although it is widely accepted that animals communicate among themselves and with human beings, the notion of telepathic interspecies communication, by telephone no less, invites skepticism. The whole subject makes people a bit nervous, in that it requires an acceptance of a totally different kind of universe than most of us grew up with, a universe fluid and without boundaries, where telepathy is a natural form of communication. But as it turns out, various and somewhat capricious psi phenomena—

psychic powers such as mental telepathy—have been validated by researchers in statistically significant tests, suggesting the deep interconnectedness of all life, something that is more than a strictly material reality.

I don't know exactly how animal communication works; I'm not even sure whether it works at all. But I have often relied on the insights into animal life it apparently provides. Gail herself was initially dubious about the whole enterprise, but she started receiving messages from animals at the shelter where she was volunteering, and when she paid attention to them, she got results. People who worked at the shelter began asking her for help with their own animals. For a year she gave animal consultations gratis, and soon thereafter she built up a large client list.

Gail's teacher, Penelope Smith, essentially pioneered interspecies communication and has trained close to one hundred people now working in the field. Penelope asserts that we're all born with the ability to communicate telepathically, but this ability tends to disappear or lie dormant once language develops, and in the absence of reinforcement. But hers lingered, and it blossomed as she began to work with it and to train others.

Often, according to Gail, communication with animals takes place through the transmission of images. When she wants to communicate the passage of time, for instance, to creatures who live in the present tense, Gail visualizes light and then darkness to signify a day, the moon waning and waxing to indicate passage of a month.

History and myth are full of examples of interspecies communication. In Native American mythology, wisdom is frequently imparted to humans by animal guides. The Bible talks of King Solomon, son of David, who "spake with beasts, fowl, creeping things, and fishes." One of the most celebrated incidents of animal communication in the Western tradition is Saint Francis's conversation with the wolf that had been terrorizing the mountain town of Gubbio, killing people as well as livestock. According to an account from the fourteenth century, Saint Francis bargained with the wolf: The townspeople would feed him, but he had to leave the townspeople alone. After this conversation, both sides honored the deal, and the wolf remains pictured on the city seal to this day. True, that conversation did not take place over the phone. But still, if the channel through which it occurred was telepathic in nature, presumably it could have taken place across distances.

When dealing with such mysteries, I tend to suspend disbelief; my goal is to see what might be revealed to me, taking heart in Keats's notion of "negative capability," the ability to be "in uncertainties, mysteries, doubts, without any irritable reaching after fact and reason." Though most of the information I received through Gail was nonverifiable, everything she told me expanded and enriched my understanding of the cats I was dealing with, added layers of complexity to their characters, and helped me empathize with their situations and see them as unique beings with distinct experiences and ways of understanding the world. These complex, independent creatures never did become transparent to me. And, true to cat nature, they never blindly obeyed my requests. (A cat will never betray itself, as one friend put it.) But Gail's ability to get through to the cats appeared to be another tool to help guide me, and I was looking for all the help I could muster. Nothing she told me ever seemed off base or proved to be inaccurate. All of the information was informative, some was amusing, and much of it was useful. The big red cat's response pierced me like a dagger.

I had first contacted Gail the summer before the cat rescue, when I was trying to figure out whether to bring my beloved furry companion, Casey, upstate with me. At the time I was enrolled in an intensive graduate summer school program, and I wasn't sure how well Casey would adapt to a temporary room or whether she'd be welcome in the dorm. During the first month-long semester, I left her with my sister while I was getting my bearings. For the entire four weeks, Casey continued to glare at Lois as if she were a catnapper and swiped at her if she got too close. Lois longed to pet her, but every time she drew near, Casey raised a paw, ready to swipe. Casey was Janet's kitty, her actions said, and no one else had rights to her. Her loyalty, even if it was overly prudish, touched me.

I weighed Casey's isolation at my sister's against the anxiety that the move might create. I considered how she'd react to the long car trips up and back. I wondered if she'd feel comfortable in a single room with strangers all around. Unable to resolve the dilemma, I called Gail, who had been recommended to me by a friend.

Gail's initial reaction, after I described the situation, was that relocating my kitty for a month was a bad idea. "Cats that old (Casey was fourteen at the time) usually have a hard time traveling and getting used to new surroundings," she said. But after communicating with Casey directly, she had a different opinion.

To talk to an animal through an animal communicator such as Gail, one first sets up a phone appointment. A communicator usually suggests that callers have a list of questions ready, a description of the cat, its setting, and the address. Somehow that information, coupled with the intelligence of the communicator, leads to the right feline informant. I wondered how such a sketchy description could actually put Gail in touch with the right animal. But one day as I successfully delivered an e-mail to a friend who had moved to new location, it occurred to me that if electronic messages can hone in on their recipients so precisely simply through the click of a few keys, perhaps telepathic messages have some equally efficient mechanism for connecting sender with receiver, even if that mechanism is not yet known to us.

Once we were ready, Gail disappeared into silence on the other end of the line for a few moments as she zeroed in on Casey. She always begins by asking the animal if it is willing to talk.

"I suppose so," said my Casey, in what Gail described as a "perky" voice.

After a little interspecies discussion, Gail reported back. "She's got her bags packed. She really wants to be with you."

Casey had told Gail she was not happy at my sister's place—she didn't find the tiny apartment very "stimulating." And she missed me. She loved me very much and was eager to join me in the country, even if it meant a long car ride.

What could be more pleasant for a devoted pet owner to hear? I packed up and set off, accompanied by intense, plaintive wailing for the hour or so it took to get beyond the hot and muggy city. But by the time we got well beyond the veterinarian's office, the usual destination she associated with car trips, and reached the tree-lined parkway heading north, into territory she had never known, Casey calmed down and seemed to take an interest in the green smells and pastoral views.

The dorm where I lived looked like an oversized clapboard house and accommodated about twenty students. Once I unpacked and let Casey loose in the room that contained many of my things and my scent, she relaxed. She seemed to know instantly that she was home. All that summer she enjoyed sitting in the window and looking out at the meadow that stretched out before her, watching the butterflies and birds darting about and the occasional dog romping by. She loved the little clumps of fresh country grass I brought her to munch on. Other people in the dorm were quite taken with her and came by with offerings of grass or catnip or toys, attempting friendship. But Casey was unrelenting, swiping at anyone who tried to touch her, faithful, as always, to my caress.

Late at night after the other students on my floor were asleep, she would sometimes wake me up and beg me to open the door so she could snoop around the hallways. Later she figured out to how to work the doorknob and would let herself out, so that when I awoke in the morning, I'd find my door wide open and Casey wide-eyed and alert, clearly proud of her night's escapades. She had always had a hard time with New York's muggy summer heat and bad air, and her adventure in the country was a big success for both of us.

I called Gail again soon after initiating the rescue, when I was feeling conflicted about taking wild animals from their homes. By that time I had caught Wily, Mimi, Foxie, and Bandit, but I hadn't seen the others for a few days. I felt anguished when I saw the terror in my captives' eyes as they crouched on the bathroom sill or sink. I thought that a talk with Gail and maybe with some of the cats still outdoors might give me a better handle on the situation. Certainly it couldn't hurt. If the cats understood what was going on, maybe they would put up less resistance, maybe they would enter the traps more readily, and maybe they would suffer less. I was also thinking about the kittens that were still locked up under the building. If they could be made to understand and agree to the necessity of trapping and come willingly, my role would be easier. And I would feel better about what I was doing.

When I explained the situation to Gail, she offered to help. In fact, she waived her usual fee (at the time, $40 per half hour) in situations dealing with homeless animals. But she cautioned me before we started that some animals wanted "to live free or die." Nor was it always possible to get through to feral cats, she said, but she offered to try. We decided to focus on the big marmalade tom, Garfield, the oldest and wisest member of the group. I wasn't actually trying to trap him—he didn't live under the building with the others and wasn't threatened by the changing rules. He roamed widely, seeming to have the whole neighborhood staked out. He appeared to be comfortable where he was, and I couldn't imagine either trapping or domesticating him. But he did pass through the courtyard every night, and if anyone could convince the rest of the tribe of the wisdom of our plan, it would be Garfield.

After making contact with the cat, Gail asked if she could call him Garfield, the name I had been using, the name the security guards had given him. "You can call me that if you like," he replied, "but that's not my name."

His real name, he said, was Aloysius.

The dignity he projected, even in that initial interchange, and his refusal to be mocked struck me forcefully. I suddenly felt guilty about all the times I had joked with the security guards about "Garfield," as if this magnificent animal could be reduced to a caricature.

Aloysius agreed to talk to us, he said, even though he didn't think it would do much good. That response, too, with its undercurrent of resignation, gave me pause.

Gail explained to him that we were trapping the members of his tribe for their own safety.

Aloysius was not exactly buying it.

"You're interfering with our right to be cats," he said.

The validity of his response and the extent to which it reflected my own ambivalence was devastating. I couldn't stand to be judged harshly, even by a cat. I felt I had to justify my actions, to make him understand. Through Gail, I explained that some people didn't like a lot of cats around. That's why their home was getting blocked off.

"It's not fair," he said. And a little later, "If you take them, I'll be all alone."

I didn't know how to respond. Gail relayed to him that the four we had already captured were safe now, and she asked Aloysius if he'd consider coming indoors, where he would be away from the rain and snow, be well-fed, and have his fleas and itches taken care of. He didn't think so, he said, but he would remain open to the possibility. We bid him good-bye. I was left feeling sad and inadequate, with no idea of how to do right by this magnificent animal. Later, while pondering where in the world a wild tom cat would have come up with the name *Aloysius*, I looked it up on the Internet. It's a Teutonic name, I discovered, meaning "famous in battle."

Donna had told me on more than one occasion that old toms made some of the sweetest pets, once they came around. "I'd love to get my hands on the big red guy," she'd said the first time I met her in person. She had come by to assess the situation and to see if she could help me nab Bear and Luna, who were still living under the building. I found Donna to be a slightly faded blonde beauty with dark circles under her eyes. Even wrapped in a big, fluffy, fake leopard fur coat, she seemed tiny in comparison to the power she had projected over the phone. We had put tuna in the back of the trap and also into the back of a big cat carrier, thinking we might be able to lure a cat in there, since they were now so trap-shy. Aloysius was lingering around the fishy smell of the food. Donna tried to talk him into walking into the large carrier.

"Come on, Aloysius," she said in a soft, low purr. "Wouldn't you like to come in from the cold and get those ear mites and fleas taken care of? Wouldn't you like to spend your golden years safe and warm with three square meals a day?" He looked battered and grizzled, with little bugs flying around his head and his eyes caked with goo. His ears were all nicked up, his long fur matted. He was bold and let us get quite close, so close we could almost reach out and touch him—but not quite. He seemed interested in what Donna had to say, but he didn't walk in.

In early autumn, about six months after the last of the courtyard tribe was captured, I stopped by to see what was going on at the feeding station in back. One of the German ladies I had met there was furtively leaving what looked like a pound of meat on the ledge between the sidewalk and the park. I asked if she had seen the big red tom. She told me Aloysius was dead, run over by a car. I was surprised by how much it hurt to hear the news, even though I knew he had lived for quite a long time on the streets. Dying quickly under the wheel of a car was, perhaps, an easier death for this creature who seemed so strong and noble than growing sick and old, and dying cold and weak and miserable in the dead of a harsh winter. It was better too, perhaps, for a warrior to die under the wheel of a car than to be killed by a younger cat in a fight.

But by the time I reached my car, tears were streaming down my cheeks. Mentally I played over our connection: I had fed this cat from time to time, watched him rear several litters of kittens, taken his family from him when they were in danger, and, in fact, trapped his consort right before his very eyes. He was probably the closest thing to a big wildcat that I'll ever have the privilege of living near and observing close at hand. His proud, leonine presence, as he sat in the park at dusk watching the evening energies take hold, was enough at times to transport me in spirit to the wide Serengeti Plain.

Later I read a rumor about stray cats in Rome that commit suicide by running under cars. I wondered if there were any truth to it and whether Aloysius might have intentionally taken that exit route.

We called on Gail during times of crises as well. One evening I came home from work exhausted, sick, and discouraged because only two of the cats were in what seemed to be permanent homes, and one of those homes was uncertain. Beautiful, shy Wily, and Luna, her monkey-faced, tortoiseshell half sister, were in temporary foster care at my sister Lois's place.

I was lying down when I got a call from Lois, who sounded equally dispirited. "What's the matter?" I asked.

"I think Wily escaped."

"How?"

"Catherine was here, and I forgot to tell her to be careful about the window. I came home, the window was wide open, and I can't find Wily anywhere. Luna is running around looking all distressed."

My sister's cleaning lady had come for the first time since Lois took the cats. Unsettled, no doubt, by the energy of a different person in the house, the unusual daytime hustle and bustle, the smell of cleaning products, and, probably most of all, the roar of the vacuum cleaner, Wily had disappeared.

"Are you sure she's not hiding somewhere?" I asked.

"I've looked everywhere."

"Did you go out on the roof?"

"Not yet," Lois said. "I don't see anything down there."

My sister's apartment has three windows overlooking a wide rooftop one floor down, with no access to the street. A cat could easily jump down, and would almost certainly survive the drop. But then it would have to negotiate a rusty jungle of industrial exhaust fans, radiator ducts, and other rooftop mechanisms that looked as if they could suck a cat in and spew out the pieces.

"You'd better try to get down there and look around," I said.

After considerable negotiation, Lois first tried to access the rooftop through the downstairs deli, but finally she ended up crawling through the bathroom window in the second-floor beauty salon. The roof was dank with puddles and debris. Night was falling, and the mosquitoes were hungry. Lois called and called, but she didn't find Wily anywhere.

"Do you think we can call Gail?" Lois asked an hour later when she returned from her mission.

I called. Usually Gail requires advance appointments. Usually she doesn't work in the evenings, but because this was an emergency, she said she would try to reach Wily as soon as she finished her dinner.

In the meantime, I cried. I had trapped this shy little kitten that I had wanted to help, I had terrorized her, and now, perhaps, she was totally displaced, lost in the cold, cruel city.

Gail called back with some information. "She's very scared," Gail said. "She's having a hard time breathing. I can feel the pounding of her heart. But I think she's in the apartment, in back of something. I see wood floors around her. She seems to be trapped." Gail had also contacted Luna, who didn't know where her playmate had gone.

My sister lives in a small one-bedroom apartment. She had already taken almost everything out of her closet to make sure Wily wasn't there, and she'd looked behind every row of books on her shelves. One of the best ways to find a hiding cat

Photo courtesy of Meredith Weiss

is to shine a flashlight into all the hidden recesses and crannies, looking for the reflected glare of the cat's eyes in the darkness. Lois had already shined the flashlight into every place she could think of, even down the improbably narrow space behind the stove, a space that could be reached only from the top of the kitchen sink and then only by taking a steep plunge into a vein of darkness just two and a half inches wide. After hearing from Gail, Lois pointed the flashlight down there once again. This time she saw the glimmer of two eyes. She couldn't reach Wily down in the narrow crevasse, but she pulled the stove out to give the cat room to maneuver and turned out the lights. Within half an hour, Wily jumped out and retreated to her usual hideaway in the back corner of the closet.

Lois had originally taken the two cats strictly as a temporary measure. She was fostering them, getting them ready for permanent homes. She didn't spend enough time at home to own cats, she said, and it was too hard to make cat-sitting arrangements when she wanted to leave town. But after that incident Lois no longer spoke of finding permanent homes for Wily and Luna.

While Wily was missing, Lois had made a pact with herself: If only she could find the kitten safe and sound, she would always take care of her. Wily's vulnerability, and the thought of her lost in the city, hiding in some dark shaft between buildings, clarified Lois's attachment to her. "By pain we learn the extremity of love," the poet Wendell Berry once wrote. My sister would learn that lesson more deeply later on.

After Wily's behind-the-stove adventure, Lois's partner, Murray, continued to talk about the necessity of training and grooming the kittens for permanent homes. Gradually it dawned on him that the cats weren't going anywhere. They had moved in to Lois's heart.

A year later, before leaving town for a short vacation, Lois had another little chat with Luna and Wily. The appointment was during the day, so Lois was speaking through Gail to Luna from the office. One of the first things Luna demanded to know before she agreed to talk was when Lois would be getting home.

Soon, Gail assured her. Then Gail told little Luna, who had been diagnosed with a congenital liver problem, that all the doctor's visits had been to figure out why she was getting so sick, and that they were over for the time being. Luna was glad to hear that, because the last few weeks had been, as she put it, "dreadful."

When she found out that Lois's friend Sarah would be taking care of her and Wily, Luna wanted to know whether Sarah would be spending the night, whether there would be a warm body in the bed to snuggle up against in the dark.

Then Gail attuned her connection to Wily, who wanted to know if someone would be feeding them every day. After assuring her that she would be fed daily, Gail probed to find out if Wily ever felt like getting a little more familiar with humans. Didn't a closer physical relationship, like the one Luna had with people and which included lots of petting and snuggling and purring, look like fun? It did look intriguing, Wily indicated, but something stopped her. She just couldn't let go. And something else bothered her: Luna sometimes disappeared. Wily associated her companion's recent overnight visits to the veterinarian's and the animal hospital as having something to do with her close contact with humans. Apparently those disappearances of Wily's only close friend disturbed her deeply. Where did Luna go? Would she come back? Wily was afraid that if she got closer to humans, she, too, might vanish into the wide unknown.

The directness of Wily's reactions and the extent to which she was ruled by fear of what she didn't understand reminded me of a passage by Temple Grandin I had read in the anthology, *Intimate Nature: the Bond Between Women and Animals*, a remarkable autistic woman who believes her skewed cognitive abilities give her insight into the animal mind. She writes:

Language-based thought is foreign to me. All my thoughts are full-color motion pictures, running like a videotape in my imagination. It was always obvious to me that cattle and other animals also think in pictures. I have learned that some people mainly think in words, and I have observed that these verbal thinkers are more likely to deny animals' thought: they are unable to imagine thought without words. Using my visual thinking skills, it is easy for me to see things from their perspective . . . I can imagine looking through their eyes or walking with four legs. It is the ultimate virtual reality system.

My life as a person with autism is like being another species: part human and part animal. Autistic emotion may be more like an animal's. Fear is the dominant emotion in both autistic people and animals such as deer, cattle, and horses. My emotions are simple and straightforward like an animal's, not deep-seated. They may be intense while I am experiencing them but will subside like an afternoon thunderstorm.

Over the years a number of my friends used Gail's services. They were always impressed by the particularity of the animal's language and its appropriateness to the animal in question. This aspect of animal communication truly baffled me. Getting into an animal's head was one thing, it seemed to me; having it spout complete English sentences or idiomatic phrases was another. I asked Gail how it worked: How could feral cats and other wild animals, who had never been around humans, have language skills?

"I can't really explain how it happens," Gail said. "Some communicators only get emotions, images, or states of mind. I am often able to translate those into words. And the language that comes out always seems particular to that being. It puzzled me at first, too. Maybe some of those animals were in human form at one time. Maybe they've gotten used to hearing human language. But if there is a collective consciousness, perhaps there is a collective language, too. If you can tap into universal consciousness, it seems you can get wisdom back." ❧

— Chapter 5 —

Finding
Good Homes

Regard it as a privilege to get in
close contact and establish a good
relationship with wild animals.

—*Penelope Smith,* Animal Talk

In retrospect, trapping was the easy part of the rescue mission. "The world is saturated with cats," one rescuer told me when I began networking to find homes for Mimi's brood, and I soon discovered she was right. Had I realized how difficult it would be to find appropriate situations for five feral cats in various stages of wildness and two skittish three-month-olds, I'm not sure I would have initiated the rescues. Indeed, I now recommend returning feral cats to the area in which they have managed to survive. But in the months following that first rescue, through luck or grace or a combination of the two, I finally got all the cats placed.

It was lucky that my sister eventually took the little tortoiseshell kitten and Wily, and that my friend Pam offered to take one of the grays right away. A fellow graduate student who lived nearby, Pam had seen the kittens in the courtyard and was sympathetic to their plight. She and her husband, John, lived in a two-room co-op with their eighteen-year-old diabetic terrier, and they wanted a cat to round out the household. They both loved animals and had owned cats before. Moreover, Pam approached everything she did in a capable and thorough way. I had no qualms about giving her one of the cats; in fact, I was grateful that she offered to take one without my stooping to cajolery or bribery. Although Pam understood from the start that a feral cat can be more of a project than a pet, I don't think any of us were prepared for the length and difficulty of the effort—an effort, though, not without rewards.

Even before Pam picked up the gray cat at Dr. Cotter's, Natasha, the doctor's wife, had observed that Bandit, as we called him, tended to express fear by losing control of his bowels. Unfortunately, Bandit scared easily. In the first month or so, he had six or seven accidents—one on the way to his new home; a few when Pam and John's ailing terrier, Suzie, barked loudly or suddenly; and others when he had to be cornered into his carrier and taken to the vet. Pam didn't complain about the mess, even though at the beginning, while Bandit was still fighting worms and getting used to a new diet, the smell was intense, especially to Pam's highly sensitive nostrils. She didn't complain when Bandit bit her badly, requiring a doctor's visit and a regimen of antibiotics. Neither Pam nor John complained, either, about Bandit's occasional vomiting in their small apartment.

But after several weeks of caring for a terrified cat that she couldn't hold or pet, a creature who usually hid under a bed, Pam, desperate for advice, called the veterinarian for help in drawing Bandit out. "Handle him every day," Dr. Cotter advised. He urged her to swaddle Bandit in a towel, then hold him firmly while stroking him gently. She gave it a try. To simplify the procedure, she shut the French doors, usually left open, that separated the apartment's two rooms. When she draped the towel around him and attempted to pick him up, Bandit demonstrated the awesome power of a terrified cat. In an explosion of fur, glass, and shit, Bandit bolted from Pam's grasp, lost control of his bowels, and, leaping for the safety of the other room of the apartment, shot directly through the closed French doors. The panes were old and thin, and Bandit hit with such velocity that he was unharmed, but cat shit and shards of glass lay strewn along the path of his flight. Pam, as shaken as Bandit, made no further attempts to hurry things along.

When a second vet suggested a behavioral approach, using food as a reward and a weapon to tame him, John would have none of it. "I think he should stay as wild as he wants for as long as he wants," he told me, winning my continued high regard. Many experts on the subject agree and advise letting feral cats set their own pace. However, three years after Pam and John adopted Bandit, he was still virtually unpettable. By that time their old terrier had died, and they'd taken in another, more affectionate cat, Noodle, a white male found wandering around the East Village. After a two-day hissing courtship, Bandit and Noodle became best friends and spent their days curled together on the couch. Now Pam had one cat she could interact with and another who was at least content, definitely safe, and gradually growing more at ease.

During the entire time I was trying to find homes for the cats, Donna stayed in close contact, giving me leads, taking me through the screening process, and most of all, encouraging me to have faith that things would work out somehow. She was a huge help, but at times she came out with statements like, "I want people to beg for these kittens," I wondered whether she hadn't set the bar a little too high. Anyway, red-haired Dave, who'd threatened us on our first night of trapping, was the only person who came close to begging, so when he grinned at me with his slightly off-kilter smile and told me he and his fiancée definitely wanted one of the cats, I didn't know how to say no. Dave claimed to know all about feral cats because his mother-in-law had taken some in, and besides, he already had a dog and a cat, so Scamper would have company. Still, I didn't quite trust him and wasn't enthusiastic about the idea of giving him a court-yard cat. Donna was even less so. Despite our misgivings, we both recognized that the cats needed somewhere to go. Scamper, the boldest of the litter, had been caged at Dr. Cotter's for over a week and Natasha kept asking when I was going to pick him up. I had no other prospects, and here was Dave, a guy who claimed he loved animals, who was out walking his dog every night, and who seemed to feel he had a right to one of the cats from our common courtyard. Who was I to turn down a viable prospect?

"Rule number one: Never give away a cat because you're scared," Donna told me when I explained my dilemma. She offered to screen Dave for me, to check out his apartment and get him to fill out the adoption form promising the cat a permanent home and responsible care. Although he had bragged that he and his fiancée together had a "six-figure income," it turned out they had almost no furniture in their large apartment. Their own cat was obese and had patchy fur, they didn't seem to have a regular vet, and worse, their windows lacked screens, one of the first things to check for with any prospective cat owner. Hundreds of cats fall from open windows each year in New York. While cats are known to survive falls from incredible heights, they are seen all too often for broken backs at animal hospitals and veterinarian's offices. Dave gave Donna a check for $60 as an adoption fee, money that would be used to help cover Scamper's neutering and shots, but Donna offered to tear up Dave's check in return for his promise to use the money to purchase window screens.

We let Dave take Scamper, the pick of the litter, because I thought that he and his girlfriend actually did love animals, whatever other failings they might have, and because Scamper was the only cat of the bunch who seemed relaxed enough around humans to be placed in such a household.

"How's Scamper?" I would ask whenever I ran into Dave in the courtyard.

"He's great," Dave would always say, but he admitted that domesticating the cat was more difficult than he had expected. Scamper hid in one room, and, although he liked the dog and the other cat, he shied away from Dave. One evening when I met Dave walking his dog in the courtyard, he ushered me to a spot where his apartment was in view so I could see Scamper four floors up, pacing back and forth at the window, keeping an eye on his old territory.

A month or two after Scamper had settled in with Dave, I left town for another session of summer school. One weekend when I returned home, I ran into Dave again. "How's Scamper?" I asked as usual. As usual Dave answered, "He's great," and proceeded to tell me about how Scamper had jumped from the window to join his friends.

It turned out Dave and his fiancée hadn't purchased the screens as they had promised. Instead they kept their tall windows closed at the bottom and open at the top, thinking that would be adequate. But one night Scamper had heard or seen or smelled his old buddies in the courtyard and didn't want to miss out on their company. He had scrambled up four feet and over the window pane, and had then fallen or leapt four stories to the ground, which, fortunately, was softer than usual, having been soaked by a recent rain.

The next morning when Dave was leaving for work, he discovered Scamper, unharmed, sniffing at the apartment's lobby doorway that faced the courtyard, clear on the other side of the building from where he had fallen. Apparently Scamper wanted to come home, and he had managed to figure out which doorway was his.

"I think he's learned his lesson," said Dave. "He seems more content with us now. I think he's happy to be inside."

"*Scamper's* learned *his* lesson!" Donna fumed when I told her what had happened. "Scamper's a cat. Dave's a thirty-five-year-old man. Who's supposed to learn something from this?

"That creepy, lying, mean-spirited, conniving, psychopathic son-of-a-bitch," she said and went on to produce a truly impressive string of invectives, more than I can remember or recreate even with a thesaurus at hand. Our reservations about Dave had been warranted, and we both winced at the image of Scamper flying out of the window into thin air. Donna had once told me that because of their poor depth perception, cats misjudge how far away the ground is. I kept thinking of Scamper in midair, realizing while in free fall that he'd made a terrible mistake, and I realized why people who screen prospective cat owners tend to be so picky.

Donna, I gathered, gave Dave quite a talking to. When the conversation was over, Dave got the screens and took the cat to a vet. "She really scared me," Dave said with that odd smile when I ran into him later. I believed him. Donna defending an animal was like a force of nature.

Donna offered to foster and try to socialize little Foxie when he was released from the hospital. A silvery blue three-month-old, Foxie had been hospitalized for several weeks with an upper respiratory infection, a condition that can be fatal for cats. Donna was crazy about the little kitten, but one of her two old cats didn't like him at all. Her studio apartment was tight even without cats. And her boyfriend, knowing how far she would go for an animal, was leery of her bringing home a third cat.

So Donna took on the responsibility of finding Foxie a home. She took Polaroid photographs of the seductive Foxie stretched out in the window, gunmetal fur shimmering in the sun. In the margins of these photos she wrote, "Loving!" "Unspoiled!" "Playful!" "Intelligent!" "Affectionate!" and, under

Foxie's image, "Foxie needs a home." He looked so sleek and alluring that I accused Donna of peddling "kitty porn."

Four or five households expressed interest. Donna made several home visits, but none of the prospective owners met her standards: One was ideal except that the woman had expensive furniture and wanted to declaw Foxie, an operation that can be so traumatic and painful to cats that it is outlawed in England. Another prospective owner seemed too young and without sufficient resources to take on a cat. A third had a rooftop onto which Foxie could possibly wander. "I can't take that kind of risk," she said. "I want a home where I can simply call every six months and hear that everything is fine."

In the end Donna kept him herself. Although the dynamics in the household were complicated—the tension of three cats jockeying for position on the bed at night, she said, suggested moves in a high-stakes chess game—Foxie became part of the family. "He's the love of my life," Donna claims when I call, every year or so, to see how they're doing.

My plans to leave town the summer after Bear and Mimi's rescue were complicated by the fact that they still resided in various corners of my apartment. I knew that a picture is often the key to finding homes for hard-to-place cats. So I made a poster, featuring a soulful-looking picture of Mimi crouched on the ledge of my bathroom window, and wrote this notice.

Sheltered outdoor position wanted
Mimi, who comes from the courtyard of a building on New York's Lower East Side, has survived three winters,

two litters, numerous dogfights, and lots of rat traps and poison. When her home under the building was boarded up, she and six of her kittens were trapped humanely, neutered, and vetted. The kittens have adapted in various ways to apartment life, but Mimi seems very uncomfortable in a human environment. Like her kittens, Mimi is strong and healthy, has tested negative for feline leukemia and FIV, and has had all her shots. Do you know of a barn or another situation for a semi-feral but very sweet kitty?

One person I had called earlier in my endless attempts at networking offered to post the sign in her upstate dress shop, and I hung others in pet stores. A month passed with not even a call. Time was running out and I was growing increasingly anxious, so I did what I sometimes do when I'm really desperate: I prayed. Then, about three weeks before I was to leave for the summer, I got my only response. That one call from Ted Pugh, who needed a cat, or maybe two, to keep the field mice out of his country place, seemed to be the miracle I had asked for.

Ever since my first rescue, I had been hoping for an indoor/outdoor situation for the feral cats. Cats are, after all, designed to live outdoors, and they seem to come more fully alive outside. Though many people argue that cats are perfectly content indoors, I thought the outdoors offered a chance for a fuller life, especially to cats used to living in the elements. My childhood cat, Butterball, had enjoyed the freedom of roaming around our suburban yard for eighteen years, fiercely attacking any dogs or cats that dared to venture into his territory. I felt he had enjoyed the best of both worlds: the safety and security of a loving family and the stimulation of the natural world he was wired for.

When I told Donna about my dream that the cats could live outdoors and have access to shelter, she resisted the idea. "That's not going to happen," she said. From the start, she was suspicious about the country place I'd found, even though it seemed to offer everything that would make a feral cat happy. Ted, who was very pleasant over the phone and receptive to taking both cats, owned a place that seemed even more ideal than anything I had visualized.

When I met him later, Ted looked as I'd imagined he would: a bearded, bespectacled, intelligent-looking guy in his fifties. After a successful acting career in New York, he and a colleague had decided to follow a dream and were now codirectors of a rural acting troupe that resided in a large, rural duplex with an outbuilding that served as another living space.

As Ted told me over the phone, the house had a large basement with a stairway leading to a first-floor solarium. A rubber cat door, already installed though inaccessible unless a plank was propped up to it, led from the basement to the outdoors. Although Ted's troupe was often off touring, his leading lady's husband would always be around to feed and look after the cats. Ted confessed to being more of a dog person than a cat lover, but he seemed to have a genuine feeling for animals. Furthermore, as he told me, the house had come with instructions from the previous owner that cats should be considered an essential part of its maintenance.

Ted's codirector lived in one half of the duplex with her husband and two luxurious-looking indoor Persian cats, which were thought to be afraid of mice, or, at any rate, showed no interest in catching them. Ted and the actors lived more or less communally in the other half of the duplex and the outbuilding, in what seemed to me like a 1960s fantasy. They spent their time creating and rehearsing wonderful theater pieces and then performing them in small towns around the Northeast and in the city. The summer I met them, they were dramatizing a piece from Ovid's *Metamorphoses,* in what was once a church in the village of Kinderhook.

I could hardly believe my luck. It seemed incredible that anyone living in the country would actually be willing to import a couple of cats from the city. But my optimism was tempered by a warning chord: things seemed a bit too perfect. Donna, who didn't seem to trust human beings much, continued to be leery of the situation and of Ted.

"He wants the cats to work for him," she huffed. "If he wants them to get rid of the mice, he's just going to have to pay them. I insist that they always have clean litter in case the weather's bad, and food and water. And they must be kept indoors until they get used to the place." Ted seemed perfectly amenable to all Donna's conditions, I told her. In fact, he seemed to agree that they were very sensible.

By this time I had become quite fond of Mimi. Though she never meowed, I felt that she and I had established our own form of communication. When she wanted to tell me something, she stared at the appropriate referent with her sad, soulful eyes. She would tell me "I could use some food," for instance, by an intense look that went from me to her food bowl and back again. Or she'd say, "The litter box could use some attention," by gazing wistfully in its direction. One evening two weeks before her departure date, she ventured out from the spot behind the dishes in my lower cabinet where she now spent most of her time and sat in full view on my counter, just a few feet away from where I was doing the dishes. Unless you've worked with a feral cat, you might not appreciate what a huge breakthrough, what a show of courage that represented. I kept talking to her encouragingly and set out a special treat so she'd know she was welcome to come out of the cupboard again anytime. But she never did.

I arranged to bring the two cats up to Ted's the week before Memorial Day weekend. On the day Ted and I had agreed on for the kitty transfer, I herded Bear and Mimi into cat carriers, no simple feat. I situated the two carriers in the back seat of the car so that the cats could see one another and possibly derive some comfort from each other's presence. As we drove the hundred miles upstate to their new home in the country, Bear and Mimi were, as usual, silent and, undoubtedly, scared. After all they had been through, they had no reason to think that anything pleasant awaited them.

Two and a half hours later I pulled into Ted's long, curving driveway and rejoiced at what I saw. The house, on the crest of a rolling hill, was surrounded by a wide, green lawn, beyond which lay an expanse of meadow and woodlands. In all directions a pastoral panorama opened up. The Catskill Mountains rose gently in the west, beyond the shimmering Hudson River, while the Berkshires rolled languidly to the east. The country road we'd driven up had had virtually no traffic and was out of earshot of the house. As I looked around, meeting Ted and his fellow actors, the situation seemed so much better than anything I could have dreamed up. Clearly someone up there (Saint Francis? My father? Bastet, the cat goddess of the Egyptians? I'm not exactly sure how these things work) had pulled a few strings.

While Ted and I surveyed the house and its cat quarters, I left Bear and Mimi in their carriers out on the lawn where they could inhale the fresh country air, take in the green smell of the grass, and attune themselves to the country sounds. The actors were wonderful. One, a rosy-cheeked German woman with lively blue eyes, had grown up on a farm with lots of cats around. She and a young man who was living in the outbuilding had already engaged in a friendly rivalry about who would be first to tame the wild creatures. It seemed that Bear and Mimi, having survived the dangers of the Lower East Side, were being delivered to a cat paradise.

Although I could hardly wait for the cats to get outside and approve of the great place I had found for them, several knowledgeable people I had talked to emphasized how important it was that the cats be confined for several weeks, perhaps months, before going outdoors. Cats, cautious by nature, had to get accustomed gradually to their new home as a source of food and security.

Alley Cat Allies, in their fact sheet about relocating feral cats, is very specific on this point. Unfortunately, I didn't have their wise directions at the time. Here is what they said:

> The animals should be kept caged for a minimum of 24 hours to orient them to a new environment prior to release into a closed barn, shed, or any other shelter which does not allow them access to the outdoors. It is mandatory that the cats come to regard the building as their permanent feeding station before they are permitted to roam from it. During their 24-day confinement period, the new caretaker must regularly visit the cats to ensure the bonding essential to successful relocation. Speaking to the cats, even if they remain hidden, helps them to overcome their ingrained fear of humans. After this confinement period the cats can be given access to the outside. Some small opening should be provided so they may enter and depart from the building at will. Daily meals in the building must be provided without fail.

Nancy, an animal rescuer who had moved upstate, also warned me about what could happen. She had brought several city cats to her place in the country and had carefully constructed a special shelter with a chicken wire pen for them. But although she thought it was cat-proof, they had all disappeared the first night, never to show up again. None of us wanted that to happen to Bear and Mimi, and Ted agreed that the cats should stay indoors for several weeks, at least.

If Donna had accompanied me, I would have avoided my biggest mistake. That mistake—and it seems like such an obvious one now that I understand feral cats better—was to let

the two cats loose in the large basement, with its cubbyholes and nooks and crannies where they could hide out almost indefinitely. In my enthusiasm to give the cats some freedom, I had forgotten a key point: Wild cats feel more secure in smaller places, places they can explore and get to know thoroughly. Then, gradually, they can expand their territory. I had forgotten how fearful cats are of anything new.

The small solarium upstairs could be closed off and, if I had been thinking clearly, would have been an ideal starting point for Bear and Mimi. There they would have seen people coming and going, and they would have begun to feel secure as they realized that the food would come regularly and that no one wanted to hurt them. Later, after they got comfortable in the solarium, they could have explored the basement. We could all have avoided a lot of anxiety. But I wasn't thinking like a cat, not then.

In my early dealings with these wild animals, I kept projecting human feelings onto them. Bear and Mimi would take to their new home immediately, I felt sure, because it had everything their old home had: underground recesses, subterranean channels, a door leading to the outdoors, and a grassy yard. I could almost see them on the lawn, chasing butterflies and field mice, having the time of their lives.

Overly eager to release the cats and see their reaction to freedom, I took the carriers to the basement and opened the doors. Nothing happened right away. Ted and I walked around the basement. By the time we got back to the carriers, Mimi had silently slinked out and promptly disappeared in the space behind a plasterboard wall. Bear was still crouching in his carrier, too frightened to venture out. The troupe had to get to an acting engagement and I needed to head home, even though Ted had graciously set up the guest room for me in case I wanted to stay over. I upended the carrier to force Bear out. He emerged in that low, crouching walk—a friend calls it swimming—that frightened cats sometimes resort to. He let out a long, lingering, plaintive yowl, which was only the second vocalization I had ever heard from him. It resounded through the basement and echoed in my heart. He let out that single, sad yowl, just like the way he had cried before he entered the trap, and then he followed Mimi's trail up into the wall.

Over the next week, I telephoned several times to check up on the cats, but I was not able to reach anyone. Anxiety had replaced euphoria by the time I finally reached Ted, about a week after I had dropped off Bear and Mimi. "Is everything all right?" I asked. "How are the kitties adjusting?"

"Well," he answered slowly, with a reserved note in his voice that bothered me. "I haven't seen them at all, which doesn't surprise me. And their food is gone every day, so I know they're eating. But they haven't used their litter box at all."

I was stunned. It had not even occurred to me that using the litter tray would be a problem. Cats almost always find litter boxes attractive; burying their droppings is an ingrained behavior that helps them hide their tracks. Every feral cat I've brought into my home—even the tiny kittens—has used the litter box consistently, with few exceptions. One of these exceptions occurred when I tried substituting a hooded model for Mimi and Wily's regular open litter pan. I walked in the next morning to find two large stools right in the middle of the bathroom floor, with the rug sort of brushed over them. The cats' message was clear: They were not about to enter that the enclosure, with its possibilities of entrapment. Another exception occurred when Bear established residence behind my stove, and Casey was asserting her territorial rights over the nearby litter box. In desperation, as I see it, he was forced into the living room, where he relieved himself on my couch.

I had assured Ted from the beginning that these cats had never had any problem with using the litter pan. What had gone wrong? I had washed out the plastic pan before bringing it up there, and I had brought along a large bag of litter: a different kind than I had been using. Maybe the new litter or the smell of the cleanser deterred them. In any case, Ted was clearly worried. If the cats weren't using the box, they were going elsewhere, and the only elsewhere that seemed likely was the dirt crawl space under the deck.

It wasn't hard to imagine what the deck would smell like, come warmer weather, if the cats were using the area beneath it as their bathroom. The house represented a longtime dream of Ted's and, obviously, a substantial financial investment. To imagine that investment diminished by the intense odor of urine and feces from two cats must have been driving him crazy.

At least he acted kind of crazy, to my way of thinking. I had asked him to please call me if there were any problems, but he hadn't even returned my calls right away. Instead he had called an animal trapper, someone country folks call when they have raccoons or skunks in their basements or chimneys. The trapper had brought over two large traps. He tried night after night to trap Bear and Mimi in the basement, with no success. I'm not sure they planned to do after that.

I was, however, demoralized. The idea was to make the cats feel comfortable and wanted and secure in their new home; the very appearance of traps would have just the opposite effect.

"Don't try to trap them anymore," I begged Ted. "I'll come up. I'll get them out of there somehow. I'll bring up some of this formula that takes the cat smell away. I'll talk to the animal communicator; somehow we'll make this work. Just please don't try to trap them anymore."

Ted's attitude seemed noncommittal. "I don't think we can catch them anyway," he said.

I called Gail. She, too, was taken aback at the thought of these exquisitely sensitive creatures facing the threat of traps in yet another environment. In any case, Gail said, eschewing the litter box was a common stress reaction. Ted had already followed Gail's suggestion and replaced the new brand of litter with the old, familiar one. He also followed Gail's suggestion to move the litter boxes to better protected spots, because cats in the act of elimination are highly vulnerable—they are, basically, disabled until they've finished. She recommended a couple of flower essence remedies that might help them with the transition. But she also said she would try to contact Bear and Mimi, try to explain how crucial it was that they use the litter tray.

Gail could only reach Mimi, who was scared and fairly non-communicative. Gail told her that the rest of the family was safe and sound in homes where they were well cared for, and that her new place, too, could be a great situation. The only thing she had to do to make it work was to use her litter box. "We'll see," Mimi said, through Gail.

But when I talked to Ted a few days later, he told me the box still showed no signs of use.

I promised Ted I'd come up in a few days to get the cats out of the crawl space. Ted and the troupe were going to be gone, but he said I was welcome to come by and let myself in.

I came armed with a gallon of an expensive product that was guaranteed to eliminate cat smell from anything. I imagined crawling on my stomach through the crawl space under the deck and liberally pouring on the liquid to eliminate the stench. I felt that I had to do whatever it would take to make this situation work. I had also brought a box of mothballs. Natasha had suggested that placing mothballs under the crawl space—the cats would abhor the camphor smell—might be a fairly nonaggressive way to persuade Bear and Mimi to move to another part of the basement.

Ted had left the house open, and when I walked in the back door leading to the solarium, the stench hit me almost like a physical force: that penetrating, ferruginous smell of cat feces. It was worse than I had imagined, and I was certain that Ted, as kind as he was, was not going to put up with it for the sake of two cats that he rarely saw and hadn't yet interacted with.

I went downstairs, armed with a flashlight and a can of cat tuna, to see if I could get a glimpse of Bear and Mimi. I wanted to see if they would respond to my voice or, more likely, to the food. As I poked my head into the crawl space, a very narrow area three feet high at the most, I didn't notice the smell that had hit me as I came into the solarium. There was no sign of the cats, either, no gleaming pupils reflecting back the light. Without success, I surveyed the many corners and cubbyholes the basement offered. Cats can vanish even in small apartments that seem to offer no hiding places whatsoever. With all the possibilities of this basement, they could be almost anywhere. I realized again how misguided my relocation strategy had been.

"There is a solution here," I said to myself, by way of reassurance. And I silently petitioned whomever up there had seemed so helpful just a few weeks earlier. I went back up to the solarium, hoping to eliminate the smell before Ted got back. I opened a little trapdoor between the floor of the solarium and the extension of the crawl space, and sniffed at the gravel below. Curiously, the smell did not seem to come from that direction. I nosed around the solarium, sniffing in corners, until I reached a large earthenware pot of soil. Bingo! Clearly Bear and Mimi had mistaken the large clay flowerpot for a litter box and had been coming up the stairs at night to use it. I took the pot outside, emptied most of the soiled dirt into the garden, mixed a cup or two of the remaining dirt into the pan of litter, and put the litter box back in the solarium, right on the spot where the flowerpot had been.

Now the solarium smelled fine. The crawl space didn't smell bad either. I was certain the cats would now understand where they were supposed to do their business. And so they did, making daily deposits in the litter box. While I was in the basement, I also removed the two metal traps that were out in full view and hid them, so these objects of fear would be out of the cats' sensory field.

─ Chapter 6 ─

Tough Guys

[Domesticated animals] became tame, not just through the fear of violence, but because they were able to form individual bonds with those who tamed them by coming to understand the social signals addressed to them. They learned to obey human beings personally. They were able to do this, not only because the people taming them were social beings, but because they themselves were.

—*Mary Midgley*, Animals and Why They Matter

After Mimi and her brood were settled in their new homes, Casey and I took off for another semester of summer school. When I returned to the city, I had nothing to do with alley cats for awhile.

Or almost nothing. With no cats in its crannies, walking through the courtyard, though pleasant enough, held few charms for me. I found myself, more often than not, avoiding it and gravitating, instead, toward the back entrance of my apartment building. Even though the scenery, if you can call it that, was drearier and more desolate when I headed out the back toward Delancey Street and the Williamsburg Bridge, that direction offered more opportunities for cat sightings.

One evening on my way out I noticed a small woman in raincoat and kerchief by the little park. I recognized her as one of the regular cat feeders and went over to greet her. She had left some food on the cement ledge and was watching as three cats—two tabby toms and a tortoiseshell female—were eating away just on the other side of the iron fence. I was able to identify the bigger cats as toms because of their wide faces and chubby jowls; the other cat I knew to be a female because her tricolor markings, a variant of calico, are found only on females of the species.

"What happened to the rest of the cats that used to live here?" I asked.

"Someone came and rounded them up," she said. "They came with nets and a truck. This one," she pointed toward the female, who was curling herself around a rung of the iron fence, "was caught in the net, but she escaped."

They had taken away six or seven cats, she told me.

When feral cats are rounded up and taken to the city animal shelter, they will almost certainly be dead in two days. Even friendly, domestic cats don't usually leave the city's Center for Animal Care and Control alive. The idea that animal catchers had come to pick up the cats was disturbing; it evoked long-buried memories of the first movie I remember seeing in a theater: *Lady and the Tramp*. At that time, as a child on the South Side of Chicago, I'd had little experience with live animals. But watching that animated band of strays—so big and wide-eyed and loveable up on the screen—trying to stay out of the clutches of the dogcatcher gave me one of my earliest intimations of how cruel and unfair life can be. Hearing mention of the animal catcher brought back an archetypal sense of menace, and I was cheered by the thought of the slinky tortoiseshell escaping his clutches.

After that encounter, I started paying closer attention to the feeding station again. I became familiar with the routines of the cats and their feeders. Once I learned the routine of the three cats, the feeding station started drawing me almost nightly. I had long harbored a vague aspiration to do fieldwork with animals, and here, suddenly, right outside my back door, I had an opportunity to do just that. It wasn't a tour to search out the Bengal tiger, as an acquaintance of mine had embarked on. But still my fieldwork fantasy wasn't all that far-fetched, since the difference between the alley cat and its cousins in the wild is mainly one of size. The thirty-seven species that make up the cat family are remarkably similar in terms of facial features, anatomy, and physiology—as well as predatory impulses and abilities. When an acquaintance was bitten while trying to break up a domestic catfight, he had a hard time convincing the emergency room staff that the damage wasn't the work of a bobcat. The degree of similarity throughout the genus is a testament to the fact that cats are a spectacularly successful evolutionary product, a design that has required little fine-tuning over the millennia. "Each one is a masterpiece," wrote Leonardo da Vinci. Mastery of predation, however, cannot compensate for loss of habitat and prey. The domestic cat, whose symbiotic relationship with humans has given it a unique evolutionary niche, is one of the few members of the cat family that is not endangered.

Tammy, the tortoiseshell whose short, wiry hair and long, lean body looked Abyssinian, was the wildest of the three cats that hung out in the little park. She was coquettish, seeming very much aware of her desirability as a single female among two toms. One tom, Nicholas, was an old and battered tabby with a gimpy leg and half a tail. He had been Aloysius's main rival, and with Aloysius gone, he seemed to be the dominant male. The other tom, Seymour, was also somewhat frayed at the ears, but appeared younger than Nicholas, although it was hard to distinguish the two from a distance. I had read that feral cat populations tend to be tabby-colored, and observing the outdoor cats was like a lesson on natural selection: Nicholas and Seymour could walk away from the feeding station, duck under the bushes or into the weeds, and literally vanish in the dappled sunlight or dusky shadows. Meanwhile, a new white and black cat had taken up residence across the street, and I could spot her from my window half a block away.

Usually the three cats seemed to get along quite well together, even though the minxlike Tammy seemed to prefer gimpy old Nicholas. But one spring evening as I was walking by, I noticed some tension between the two toms. With Nicholas standing a few feet behind him, Seymour was chomping industriously at some food on the ledge. Meanwhile, Tammy was swiping lightly at Seymour, apparently wanting a turn at the food, but he ignored her. Compared to Nicholas, who hobbled badly and was losing his fur, and whose left cheek was like one large scab, Seymour appeared hale and hearty.

In his own time and on his three good legs, Nicholas half swaggered, half limped over to the food, and it was at this point that I caught the air of tension between the two. Cats have a range of signals through which they can communicate to each other quite effectively: at least nine distinct facial expressions can combine with sixteen different body postures and tail movements to convey a wide range of emotions and responses. The signals include different positions of the whiskers and ears—forward, back, or flattened—and a rounding or narrowing of the eyes.

Not an expert on this, I surely missed much of what was going on between Nicholas and Seymour. But I did notice that Nicholas was acting different than usual—more perky, somehow, more alert. Seymour, a few feet in front of him, started to crouch, shrinking visibly. Then Nicholas let out a low, scary yowl, a sound that seemed to emanate from somewhere deep within, a sustained, guttural vocalization with resonant undertones like a Tibetan chant. That went on for maybe three minutes. A man leaned out over the rail of the second floor fire escape. "They do that every night," he called down.

Seymour was displaying submissive behavior. He was angling away from Nicholas in slow motion as if this would keep him from being noticed, backing away in that furtive, low gait cats use when trying to make themselves inconspicuous. But Nicholas did take notice. His short, scarred ears were perked forward, his hair stood on end.

Then in a flash, so fast that I couldn't see what happened first, the cats were in a rip-roaring fight, flapping back and forth in a fierce embrace. Then, just as suddenly, they were apart—and then in another instant, Nicholas sprang at Seymour. Nicholas's sudden, powerful lunge astonished me. If I hadn't witnessed it, I never would have believed this old and arthritic cat capable of such strength or agility.

"They do that every night," the man called down again from the fire escape. "The only way to stop it is to throw water on them."

I regretted I didn't have some water handy because I was afraid of the damage they might do as they tore at each other. And then, as quickly as it started, the fighting ceased. I'm not sure who won, if anyone did. Nicholas's scabbed cheek was bleeding as he limped slowly back toward the building, his half-tail curled between his legs. Seymour was walking off slowly, too, at another angle. Then Nicholas rubbed his scabrous cheek and his battered body in the dry dirt of a bare part of the lawn, rubbing and half-rolling in it as if he had run into a patch of catnip. Seymour watched from a distance, and then he and Nicholas took up positions on opposite sides of the little sidewalk. Tammy sat down at a point directly between them; later she walked off in Seymour's direction. Satisfied with this evening's observation of cat behavior, I headed upstairs.

I started seeing this little band quite regularly, and I got to know their habits. Tammy was the wild one. One of the feeders nicknamed her "The Paw" because of her tendency to bat at humans who came too close to her dinner. Seymour was friendly—he must have been someone's pet once. He would wrap himself around my legs and nudge my hand with his cheek to get me to pet him. I was afraid to touch Nicholas: he seemed too tough to handle.

One evening as I approached with food, Seymour sidled up to me and rubbed his face against my leg, marking me with pheromones from the glands on his forehead. I recognized this as a form of cat flattery: Seymour was signifying submission and marking me as the dominant one. I sat down on the curb, and he let me caress him on the head and around the ears. To see whether he could be handled easily, I tentatively put my hands around his belly. He reacted to the pressure: stiffened and slid out of my grasp. But it was a friendly maneuver—he didn't seem overly unsettled by our encounter; he just had other things to do. Seymour headed across the alley, went directly to the spot under the chain-link fence where there were a couple inches of clearance, and slipped under.

When I went upstairs, Casey started to greet me in her usual dignified manner. Catching a whiff of the scent on my pants, though, she became animated. Her nose was like a little vacuum cleaner, taking short, quick inhalations as it ran up and down my pants. She sniffed vigorously at all the spots where Seymour had rubbed, alerted by this new and strangely powerful smell—the scent of a red-blooded male. Her expression was concentrated and her nostrils flared a bit. Her attentiveness to that scent and the quiver in her nose gave me an idea: Casey might like a boy cat. Even though she had been neutered long ago, maybe she needed some masculine energy in her life. Maybe Seymour would make a good companion for her: older, not too playful, and not handsome or shrewd or manipulative enough to compete with her charms.

But I was cautious. First of all, Seymour seemed relatively happy outdoors. I was more concerned about catching Tammy, who had given birth to several litters already and who might well be pregnant again. I thought I should trap her, get her spayed, and release her back to the little park she had called home for several years now. And old Nicholas, with all his injuries it seemed like he should be the first to come in from the cold. Trying to sort out the best course of action, I called on Gail to see whether I could learn anything using her skills. By this time it was hard for me to make a move without gathering all the information I could from the cats. That's how I found out their names—Nicholas, Seymour, and Tammy—names that somehow captured their distinct personalities better than any names I was likely to have come up with.

Gail made contact with Seymour, the friendlier of the two toms, and she asked whether he'd be willing to come indoors where it was warm and safe and where he'd never go hungry. He said he wouldn't mind giving it a try to see if he liked it, and that Nicholas wouldn't mind either. But not Tammy. She was too wild.

Gail told Seymour not to be afraid of me; I was to be trusted. She told Seymour I was on his side, that I wouldn't hurt him, and that if he saw me with boxes, he should go in willingly. She didn't get into the details of the neutering process, but said I would make it so there wouldn't be too many kittens around.

A week later, on a dusky Sunday evening, all three cats rushed toward me as I headed to the back entrance of the apartment complex. Apparently the regular feeders hadn't shown up. This dry, not-too-cold night, with hungry cats, seemed to promise perfect trapping conditions. I told the cats to wait right there and dashed up to my apartment for food and gear. I brought down the trap to try for Tammy, who seemed so hungry. I also brought down a large cat carrier. I wanted to see if Seymour might actually follow Gail's instructions.

The cats nosed around the trap and sniffed at the food in the carrier. At first I didn't put the food far enough back in the trap, so Seymour was able to enter and munch away without the trap-door snapping. Nicholas and Tammy gave the trap and the carrier a wide berth—they were hungry but not foolhardy. But after a few minutes of sniffing around, Seymour walked right into the big cat carrier for the tuna I had placed inside. I let him get fully engaged in eating and then shoved his butt in and slammed the carrier door shut. Seymour continued to enjoy his food for a few moments. When he finished, he tried to get out and, realizing his exit was blocked, heaved himself at the door over and over, back and forth, until I covered the carrier with a towel. He never meowed.

I wasn't sure what to do next, so I called Vera, a neighborhood ally. She was full of advice on where to take him for neutering and how to treat patches of ringworm. When I told her he seemed comfortable in the bathroom, as if he had once been a housecat, she said, "You shouldn't put him back; not a friendly cat like that. Anyway, you should let him rest up a few days before taking him in to be neutered, so it won't be so traumatic."

Delaying the operation seemed right to me for several reasons. First of all I was a little afraid of Seymour and wasn't sure how to get him back into the carrier. Although he enjoyed being petted, whenever my hand strayed toward his stomach, he turned his head and took a nip at the air, as if in warning.

And then there was his deep fatigue. He seemed too tired to be scared, too tired to be curious, too tired even to care about the other feline presence in the house. He seemed more tired than hungry. This was, after all, the end of winter, and survival out on the streets in the cold, damp weather with an uncertain food supply must have sapped almost all his strength.

For the next week Seymour continued to sleep. He ate everything I gave him, used his litter box, submitted to my brushing and petting, and occasionally made eye contact with me. But mostly he just slept behind the toilet, looking up without interest when I came in to use the bathroom.

Initially I thought it would be hard to keep him in the bathroom for a week, but he didn't seem to mind; he didn't even seem very interested in exploring. He didn't bother to jump up on the window ledge, which had been a favorite spot of my other captives. Each day I would pet him, and each day he seemed to enjoy it a little more, tilting his cheek up toward my hand so I could stroke harder. But he seemed deeply fatigued.

Casey was curious at first, more curious than angry. After Seymour urinated, his pungent, male smell filled the bathroom and drifted out when I opened the door. When I was washing my face or taking a shower, I sometimes left the door open so Casey could have a look at him. She stared, hissed occasionally, and sniffed around at his litter box. Seymour, implacable, observed her from the corner of the bathroom he'd adopted.

After he had been in my bathroom for a week, I took Seymour to see Dr. Cotter and stayed with him throughout his examination, during which he was both well behaved and cooperative.

"He sure seems like he's used to being around people," said Dr. Cotter, who showed no hesitation or fear about handling Seymour. He palpated Seymour's torso, cleaned out his ears, wiped his eyes, and took a blood sample from his paw. "He looks pretty good for an outside cat. A few scars, a few broken teeth." Dr. Cotter estimated Seymour to be three or four years old.

I waited in the lobby while Seymour was anesthetized and neutered and while his feline leukemia and FIV tests were being run.

After awhile, Natasha called me back into the room.

"He doesn't have feline leukemia," said Dr. Cotter. "But he tested positive for feline AIDS—FIV."

Feline immunodeficiency virus, I was told, is a lot less contagious and less virulent than feline leukemia, which can weaken and kill cats in six months to a year. Like the HIV virus, FIV doesn't last long outside of the body. It spreads through bodily fluids, primarily, it is thought, during bloody catfights. FIV suppresses a cat's immune system, so its victims fall prey to other diseases. But with good care, Natasha said, FIV-positive cats have lived to be eighteen years old.

Seymour was still under the effect of the anesthesia, and, perhaps for that reason, he was both docile and extremely affectionate when I brought him home. I took advantage of his drug-induced calm to bond with him. I locked Casey in my room and opened Seymour's carrier. He walked unsteadily into the back corner of my hall closet, where I was able to pet and brush him while he purred like crazy, rolling around under my hand. It was the first time he had been so responsive. "Now what do I do with you?" I asked Seymour, realizing that even if I had Casey's approval, I couldn't expose her to FIV. "No wonder you're so tired all the time."

While Seymour was still drugged and limp, I carried him like a baby back to the bathroom. I called Vera, who had replaced Donna as my coach. When I told her about Seymour's FIV, she brought me some herbs and medications to give him: Echinacea (half a capsule every day), Pau d'Arco (half a capsule every other day), vitamin C (daily), and brewer's yeast to make it all go down.

The next week I wormed Seymour and began giving him his herbal medications. Although he still slept a lot, he started taking a more lively interest in his surroundings. He'd look expectant when I came in the bathroom first thing in the morning and again ten or twelve hours later, after work. A couple of times he even let out a faint meow.

Although he finished every plate of food I gave him, he always approached it with a certain calculated nonchalance. Instead of simply walking over to his bowl, he would casually stretch his front legs out in the general direction of the food, and then edge his hind legs up to meet them, ending up a little closer to the bowl. Then he'd act like he might have been saying, "Well, as long as I'm so close to the bowl, I'll just see what we have here."

I tried to give him some attention every time I used the bathroom—but quietly, so as not to arouse jealousy in Casey. He began to enjoy the contact more and more, purring as I stroked his back and scratched under his ears. I brushed him and brought in little toys, which he ignored. Every evening when I came home from work, I found myself increasingly eager to greet him and see how he was doing.

Late one evening I saw Tammy and Nicholas, tails raised high, trolling the sidewalk for handouts, which meant that the regular feeders hadn't been by. Since I happened to have a can of cat food with me, I opened it and put it out for them to eat. As they chomped away, I tried to pet Nicholas, just to see how he'd react. He didn't move away from my hand or jump as if electrified, as Mimi and Wily had when I first tried to touch them. He just went on eating. But Tammy made no effort to hide the fact that she did not appreciate my attentions toward Nicholas. She started batting at my hands with her front paws as if to say, "Stay away. He's mine. You may have Seymour, but don't try anything with Nicholas."

Seymour's sojourn with me lasted about six weeks. The strain of taking care of two cats and trying, not always successfully, to keep them apart, was wearing on me, and it was wearing on Casey, too. She'd grown icy and withdrawn. She glared at me from her perch in my bedroom every time she saw me taking in food to Seymour. I found myself sneaking into the bathroom to feed and pet him.

I didn't like to keep Seymour completely isolated in the bathroom, so I would often open the door and put a stepladder in the doorway to serve as a barrier, part physical, part symbolic. As long as I was up and about, the two cats seemed to respect the boundary. But when I dozed off a couple of times, I awoke to the terrible sound of angry yowls and claws thrashing against the wood. By the time I got to the cats, they were locked together in a whirl of energy, and fur was literally flying across the room. I managed to break up the first fight before Casey got hurt, but the incident made me seriously consider how I would feel if my faithful companion contracted FIV from Seymour—a sweet guy, but something of an interloper nonetheless. The second fight was even more serious. When it was over, I couldn't find Casey, but then from the kitchen I heard a deep, foreign sound. Casey was behind the garbage basket under my sink, growling in a low tone that I had never before heard from her. The fur on her back was still standing up. "Casey," I said remorsefully. "Are you okay?" She growled more loudly.

I tried to pet her, but she hissed and swiped at me, claws flashing. Her ears were bent back. "How could you let this happen to me in my very own house?" she seemed to ask with her flickering, narrowed eyes.

Casey wouldn't let me come near her for an hour or so, and even later on that day she wouldn't let me hold her or stroke her. By bedtime, when her attitude had softened, I gave her a fairly careful inspection and was glad not to find any open wounds on her body. She did seem sore in a few places, bruised, I imagined, from the pressure of Seymour's powerful hind legs.

I wasn't sure who had started the fight, but I suspected it was Casey and was quite impressed by her chutzpah, her willingness to go after this big, tough, street-fighting guy. She was half his size and probably four times his age, but she had been fortified by the instincts of the female of the species defending her home turf. "An animal claiming a specific territory functions more decisively and confidently than one on changing or unfamiliar ground," I read in Myrna Milani's book *The Body Language and Emotion of Cats*. "Animals defending a well-known territory may also receive a psychological boost from possession." Casey did have the home advantage.

Before the fight I had imagined that a two-cat household might be possible; after the fight it seemed out of the question, and I started to look in earnest for a home for Seymour. I called a number of people with FIV-positive cats, networked with many of my cat contacts, checked with a number of shelters, and sent out e-mails. No one wanted a cat with FIV. One April morning after another bad fight, I decided to put Seymour back outside. The cold weather was over. He was fattened up and well rested, his fur fluffy and shiny. He had been wormed and treated for fleas, and his ears were clean. Most important, he was neutered, which meant he would have one less reason to get into fights and spread his virus.

When the time came to put him in the carrier, though, Seymour balked at being pushed inside. He was quiet as we descended in the elevator, but he started meowing as we went through the back gate. I took him to the feeding station and opened a can of food before unfastening the carrier door. I had expected Seymour to go right for the food and to linger around me, rubbing against my legs as he did whenever I came into the bathroom.

I had expected him to display some sense of conflict. But he didn't even stop to sniff at the Premium Feast I had put down for him, or pause to say good-bye. He just went galloping off toward the little niche where his friends came in and out of the basement, and disappeared through the window. It was the only time, except when he was fighting, that I had seen him move so quickly. I felt like the strains of "Born Free" should be playing in the background. I hoped his cohorts would remember him and welcome him back.

I may have been a bit disappointed, on one level, that Seymour had left me without a backward glance. But in a deeper way, I was thrilled. Who knows how he passed the nights outdoors, but it must have been more exciting than looking out across the white hexagonal tiles of my bathroom. For a few weeks after I released him, I didn't see him at all and was heavy with guilt. Then one night I came home to find him hanging out with Nicholas and Tammy, and after that they were a regular little gang like before. Often Seymour was very friendly, nuzzling me softly, asking to be stroked. But there were a couple of occasions when I had found a viable prospect for adopting him, and I tried trapping him again. The moment he saw me with a trap or carrier, he trotted off in the opposite direction with a frightened look on his face. I believed then that he had chosen life on the wild side.

Toward the end of the summer I started fretting about what would happen when the cold weather set in. The window that gave easy access to the boiler room had been sealed shut again, closing off the cats' access to shelter from the elements. I had noticed a few small openings in the screened-up windows that Tammy, the smallest and most agile member of the group, could squeeze into. Once she got through the opening, though, there was a precipitous drop—sixteen feet or more—to the cement floor of the boiler room. Tammy managed to negotiate it. But I was sure the jump would be too treacherous for the arthritic Nicholas to attempt, and I never saw him try. Instead, he hung out in the bushes and weeds.

Richard had told me about a hut that he had built for a cat he'd been feeding in a vacant lot near his apartment, and one day I asked if he would build one for Nicholas and Seymour. I thought I could hide it in the weedy lot across the alley from the feeding station, which seemed to be a hunting ground for the cats. Richard immediately agreed, and we set off for the building supply store. Before going in, Richard took out a pad of paper and a pencil and drew up a little plan. That's when things started to get complicated.

I thought the hut should have two doors, so the cats could never be cornered inside by a dog or a human with a mean streak.

Richard thought that each door should have a wind wall, an extra hallway on each side to block the wind. Suddenly the plywood structure was getting rather big and heavy to be considered portable.

"Maybe it doesn't need a floor," I suggested.

"Oh, no," said Richard. "It has to have a floor. Otherwise it will get cold and wet in there."

"Maybe we could install cat doors instead of wind walls," I proposed, and Richard liked that idea.

There was a pet store just down the block, so I went in to check the prices. Twenty-five dollars per door—fifty bucks for the doors alone. It was beginning to seem pretty expensive for an experimental structure that might get removed at any time.

"What about a couple of shingles instead of a cat door?" I asked Richard. "If we nail them at the top, the cats could push them back and forth."

Richard was amenable to the idea. But after a pause he added, "Of course, the thing you've got to worry about is snow."

"We don't get that much snow in the city these days," I said. "And I could keep watch."

"But you're out of town sometimes," said Richard. "I don't like the idea of them getting trapped. Maybe I should build it on legs."

I wasn't too sure about that. "I think it ought to be kind of inconspicuous, so no one will mess with it. Maybe I could put it on a few bricks."

"I could paint it with a camouflage pattern," Richard offered.

"I think just rough-cut plywood is better. If it looks like a pile of junk, no one will question it."

The more we pondered the architectural ramifications of our cat hut, the more we thought that a nice simple wooden box, if we could find one, might fit the bill. Then Richard mentioned he had heard that large Styrofoam coolers with holes cut in them make good cat shelters because the material is so insulating. So we left the building supply store and headed for Kmart. They were out of coolers for the season.

"That's okay," I said. "I'll look for one around town this weekend."

When you scavenge for building materials, New York streets prove surprisingly rich. By the middle of the next week, I had come across a terrific plywood platform several inches high. And a few days later, I spied a Styrofoam box that had been used to ship steaks. I glued the top and bottom together, cemented the whole thing to the platform, and cut a small doorway in one corner. Presto, a dandy little cat bungalow. Since the platform was about twice the size of the house, the place essentially had a wood porch. I put a soft pad and some catnip inside, and Nicholas soon took up residence. Later when I started fantasizing about a freak snowstorm, I punched airholes near the top so no one would suffocate.

By the time the weather turned cold, each cat seemed to have a special place. Tammy had a way to get into the basement, and Nicholas usually stayed in the little cottage I had made for him. Seymour mainly hung out in the weeds nearby. When food arrived, the three cats, each coming from a different direction, converged at the feeding station. I used to wonder how they all knew dinner had arrived. Then one evening after putting some food down, I went across the alley to create a little lean-to for Seymour, and I saw Tammy wander over to Nicholas's spot in the weeds. I try not to anthropomorphize unduly, but it sure seemed like she was calling him to dinner.

Nicholas was moving slowly by then. He looked and sounded worse than ever. His scarred legs appeared thin and arthritic, his fur was getting sparse, his head was always full of mucus, his breathing was labored, and his nose was bloody. But if Seymour ever tried to horn in on his food, Nicholas still seemed ready to spar. Even in his weakened condition, Nicholas exerted his dominance. I marveled at his toughness.

As winter approached, Nicholas developed a nasty infection on his face, from a puncture wound just above his nostrils. His nose was swollen to three or four times its usual size, totally altering his profile. The wound appeared ready to burst. As the infection grew worse, he became more friendly toward me. I'd bring his food right up to him in his little hut, and he'd limp over, wanting to be petted and rubbed. As he looked up sweetly into my eyes, I got the distinct impression that he was asking for help. The infection looked like it might be the end of him, so I abandoned my earlier scheme of leaving him outdoors, and asked Carol, who had been urging me to pick him up, to help me. As Carol grabbed him by the scruff of the neck, I pushed his legs together, and we managed to drop him into a carrier. When the door closed, Nicholas hurled himself back and forth for several minutes, breaking open the inflamed and suppurating wound. By the time he calmed down, the door to the carrier was covered with blood and a solid white mass of tissue about the size of an almond was dangling from the metal. Carol collected the tissue in a paper towel to show the vet.

Nicholas looked so bad that I was afraid the vet might recommend euthanasia. Carol had already made me promise that I wouldn't allow it. But Dr. Moscovich seemed quite taken with Nicholas. "Look at you, you old gentleman," he kept saying, as he gently looked Nicholas over. "What have you done to yourself?" Nicholas seemed remarkably calm, considering how suddenly he had been thrust into this new environment. He didn't struggle while the vet drew blood, shot him up with antibiotics, and prodded his torso for abnormalities. The vet was amazed to find no ear mites or fleas.

Nicholas's alpha male status seemed all the more amazing to me when the vet opened his mouth, and we saw that he had hardly any teeth left—just one toward the front and a couple on either side toward the back. And he had a BB pellet lodged in one leg, which had healed crooked. When I saw how relaxed Nicholas was with the vet, I thought he must once have been someone's housecat. Or else he was just very sick and tired—or else he understood that we were simply trying to help him.

Dr. Moscovich kept Nicholas for six days. He put hot compresses on the wound, drained and sutured it, administered antibiotics, and, when the cat was feeling better, neutered him. I was worried about how much it would all cost, but when I got the bill, I found that the doctor had given me a huge break. I was only charged for the office visit, neutering, and medications— the hospital stay and Nicholas's daily care was free.

When I brought him into my bathroom, his new temporary quarters, brave old Nicholas was initially afraid to come out of his carrier. He just stretched out his neck like a tortoise and peered tentatively at the white tile and porcelain fixtures. But by morning he was out and about, meowing so desperately to be fed that I felt obliged to bring him a platter of food even before I made myself coffee.

Overnight, Nicholas seemed to have been transformed from a tough, street-fighting tom into an adoring lap cat. Instead of being mad at me for putting him through so much, he seemed to have fallen in love with me. Every time I entered the bathroom, he rose and approached me for petting and scratching. As I scratched under his ears and chin, he'd stare searchingly into my eyes, purr with a kind of gurgle, and offer me one slightly mangled paw. His meow had a short *a* sound, *maa-a-a-a*, like a little sheep. His appetite was enormous. As soon as I put a plate down, he'd go for it, noisily and urgently. And if he hadn't finished the food before I walked into the room the next time, he would go back over to it and eat eagerly again, as if to show me what a good guest he was. Casey, who had simply ignored a pair of feral kittens I had taken in briefly between Seymour and Nicholas ("They were no trouble at all," she had told Gail), was furious to find that she now had another serious rival for my attention. I felt like she could read my mind and could see my emotional energy seeping out in another direction.

A close friend of one of the regular feeders agreed to take Nicholas. Until now she had resisted getting a cat, so the fact that he had FIV wasn't a problem. Although he only stayed in my bathroom for a week, when he was gone I found myself missing him terribly. His new owner said he followed her around like a little dog and was always grateful for affection. Occasionally, she said, a quick movement would scare him and he'd suddenly hiss and lunge, but with no teeth he couldn't do much damage. After all those years outside—Vera remembered seeing him around the neighborhood for six years or more—and with so much to watch out for, BB guns, dogs, and moving parts of machinery, it must have been difficult for Nicholas to feel totally secure. ☘

— Chapter 7 —

Luna and Wily

An ordinary housecat weighs six to nine pounds, is soft, warm and yielding, and when held against the chest feels very much indeed like a human baby; or at least it does until it puts out its claws. But the tactile resemblance isn't the only resemblance. Like a human baby, a cat has a high voice, a small chin, large eyes, and a head of short hair that stands on end. Such powerful auditory and visual stimuli trigger atavistic care-giving behavior in our kind.

—Elizabeth Marshall Thomas,
Tribe of the Tiger

Photo courtesy of Lois Jensen

"I saw another little tortoiseshell cat down at the feeding station," I told my sister one day. "She looks a lot like Luna."

"Does she have violet eyes?" Lois asked. Her Luna had been a slender tortoiseshell with the lines of an Egyptian cat sculpture. She had a small, chiseled head, enormous ears, and pale violet eyes. Her face had a pensive, sometimes worried look, exaggerated by darker brown markings where furrows might have been.

Luna had often cocked her delicate head to one side, as if she were seeking to comprehend what was going on around her. Her body and legs were long and wiry like those of a thoroughbred horse.

When Lois took her to the veterinarian's office or the animal hospital—places she had frequented altogether too often—Luna never failed to elicit comment: What an unusual cat. What a beautiful cat. "She's an odd cat," said the vet at New York's Animal Medical Center emergency room. "I love odd cats," she was quick to add.

Luna had been hyper that night. As we waited outside the emergency room, one moment she'd want to be held and the next moment she wouldn't. I would place her back in the small carrier, where she'd stay for a minute before popping her head up like a kitty-in-the-box. She was on the tail end of another one of her episodes, or seizures as we were calling them by then. Although her eyes were no longer dilated and her panting had stopped, she was restless, unable to relax. Never a timid cat, she seemed more curious than scared. She was unafraid of the big dogs in the waiting room. Unafraid of the veterinarian. Unafraid of the clinical surroundings and smells.

"Some cats are just regular pets," a clairvoyant friend had told Lois. "Others come from another planet—they're aliens in fur coats. They're the ones that have so much to teach us." Although I'm not convinced about the whole concept of interplanetary interspecies habitation, if any cats are indeed extraterrestrial beings, I would bet that Luna was one of them.

"She was something, wasn't she?" Lois sometimes asks. I nod.

She started out as Moondance, named for the wild, ecstatic leaping I witnessed on the moonlit night when I had trapped her mother. But Lois didn't think the name rolled off the tongue easily enough, nor did she think my alternative, Monkeyface, did justice to this exquisite creature. She renamed her Luna, but often ended up calling her Loonie.

She had been a tricky one to catch, staying clear of the trap-door and hanging out under the building with her big brother Bear long after the others from Mimi's litter had been rescued. When I finally captured the elusive kitten, I was all excited about the mother and child reunion that would take place in my bathroom. Of course I knew that the kitten would be somewhat traumatized from the trapping itself. But I envisioned a tremendous sense of relief—perhaps even celebration—when she saw Mimi and Wily. Luna would immediately realize that everything was going to be all right after all, that there was, in fact, life after the courtyard, and that everyone was safe and warm with these human guardians.

But that's not what happened. When we brought the little kitten upstairs, she looked pathetic, a tiny, skinny, trembling thing with part of her pink tongue protruding from her mouth. After we transferred her to a carrier, I left the door open so she'd have all night to reunite and cuddle with Mimi and Wily. But the next morning I found Luna just as I had left her, trembling and alone at the very back of the cage, a bit of her tongue still pushing out through her mouth. There were no signs of the happy reunion I had envisioned, no signs, even, of recognition.

Natasha and Donna had warned me this could happen: once kittens are separated from their mother, the maternal bond, so strong initially, quickly disappears. This aspect of cat behavior was so counterintuitive for me that I hadn't quite been able to grasp it. With their wide, intelligent eyes and expressive faces, cats seemed so human in some ways that I found it hard not to anthropomorphize. How could they forget, and so quickly, members of their own tribe, with whom they'd recently been so close? I reasoned that perhaps this was an adaptive trait developed to lessen stress caused by the frequent death and disappearance of kittens in the natural world.

I dropped Luna off at Dr. Cotter's that first morning for her checkup and shots. When I came back to see her that night, she looked even worse than she had earlier. Her tongue was protruding farther, one eye was bulging out, her skinny body was shaking, and her head was swinging slightly from side to side. "Is she okay?" I asked. "She looks terrible."

"She might have a slight neurological problem," said Natasha. Luna's littermate, Foxie, had a bit of an irregularity in his eye, a "jelly eye" as Natasha called it. The mother might have had an infection or some other problem during pregnancy that left these two kittens a little less than perfect. In retrospect, I think Luna must have been having an early episode, a buildup of toxins due to her malformed liver. But at this point we didn't suspect anything of the kind.

When Luna had first been placed in the vet's metal cage, she had run round and round furiously, looking for an exit route. Failing to find one, she finally settled for a spot in the back of the cage, as far as possible from the outside, human world. Unlike Mimi and Wily, whom I usually found cringing under the newspaper lining the bottom of their cages, Luna stood erect, front legs stiff, in a posture suggesting defiance, even as her body quaked and it appeared that she could not possibly remain upright for long.

The next day the kitten was to go to my sister's, who had agreed to foster her, after some persuasion. When Lois and I went to pick her up after work, Luna looked a little better. Her pink tongue was now protruding only slightly from her mouth, making it look as if she were trying hard to concentrate. Lois thought she looked wise beyond her ten weeks. As we rode home in the cab, Luna buried her head in my neck, undoubtedly terrified by the sights and sounds of the city careening past. She clung to the warmth and pulse of another living being, unfazed, for the moment, that the being was human.

Lois was quite taken with the restless, spindly kitty. It was her first experience with a young kitten, and she felt like a new mother bringing home a baby without a set of instructions. She wasn't quite sure what to expect or what she was supposed to do with Luna. Natasha had recommended starting her off in the bathroom, so that she could first get used to a small territory. When wild kittens are let loose in the house right away, they tend to ferret out elusive hiding spots and to stay hidden, which can stall, or sometimes halt, the socialization process. Luna seemed to be about two and a half months old—a few weeks beyond the ideal age to get kittens comfortable with humans, but still young enough to be somewhat malleable. Giving kittens lots of handling when they are from five to eight weeks old makes for the most affectionate pets.

Since Lois's bathroom door didn't close tightly, she put a box of books in front to secure it. She was late getting back from work after the kitten's first day at home. Murray, who was coming over to meet the new member of the household, got there first. By the time he arrived, Luna had managed not only to pry open the door slightly but also to squeeze into the cardboard box between the books.

Now she was lying on a rumpled towel in the box, her tongue out, her head shaking. When Murray picked her up, she clung to him, again probably out of terror. Murray had even fewer clues about what to do with the little creature than Lois did, and he wasn't completely sold on the notion of fostering one of my cats, so he just put her back in the bathroom. By the time Lois got home, Murray had devised a web of string to secure the door.

That first week Luna was still quite wild, hiding from everyone but Murray and Lois. However, she took the new human environment in stride. Except when she fell asleep, exhausted, on a shoulder or a lap, she was very alert, eyes constantly roving, nose always sniffing. When I picked her up, she'd investigate my face by sniffing my mouth, nose, and eyes. Her face would come so close that I could feel her warm, moist breath and her whiskers brushing lightly against my cheek.

From the beginning, Luna had a voracious appetite and what seemed to be a very high metabolism. She'd use her front paws like hands to bat around the various fluffy toys that Lois and Murray brought home or to scoop dry morsels out of the bowl so she could eat them directly off the floor. Cat toys were strewn about the apartment, and Luna would amuse herself for hours with the dangling stuffed mice and feathers that Murray had hung from a doorframe. Early on she'd seized upon the bed as the best place to sleep at night, and, once ensconced there, she kept Lois awake by sitting near her head, pawing and patting at her hair. "She acts like Lois is a big cat," Donna told me. "It's a compliment."

"Wouldn't it be nice if Luna had someone to play with?" I asked Lois after she'd had the kitten for a couple of weeks. By this time, the last of Mimi's tribe had been captured, and three very scared, very wild cats were sharing the hiding places in my house. Casey was getting increasingly perturbed by the new-comers. Lois agreed to take timid little Wily off my hands on an emergency basis.

By the time Wily arrived at Lois's, Luna had become quite comfortable in the apartment. She was intrigued when a new arrival took up residence in the bathroom. At first, shy Wily ventured out of her carrier only when no one was around. Luna often sat in front of the carrier looking in, her head tilted quizzically to one side as if to ask, "Why don't you come out and play?" When that tactic failed, she joined Wily in the carrier.

After two days, Wily did emerge from the bathroom, only to vanish immediately. Lois finally found her wedged in an improbably tight spot behind some record albums. For a few days, Wily remained hidden in similarly invisible spaces. Then one morning Lois woke up to find the two little cats curled up together under the bed.

From that time on they were fast friends. At first Murray worried they spent too much time in their lair under the bed. Murray was still taking the fostering part of the arrangement seriously. He was concerned that if the cats hid out together, this behavior would reinforce their feral nature: they would get wilder and wilder, and be harder to socialize and adopt out. He talked about blocking off the space under the bed, so Luna and Wily would be pushed into visibility and forced to interact with people. "Our job is to turn them into nice housecats for someone," he said. Lois and I looked at each other and said nothing.

Murray worked on other fronts to ensure the kittens' adopt-ability, as well. He built a beautiful scratching post by coiling a length of rope around a twenty-four-inch-high four-by-four, which he mounted on a wide base, stenciling "Amalgamated Cats" in bold letters along one side of the rope-covered upright. The cats ignored it, preferring to shred Lois's small sofa. (Later, Lois found a double-sided tape that effectively kept the cats from scratching, but by that time the couch was ruined. Declawing was not an option.) Lois wasn't much of a discipli-narian. In view of her indulgent attitude toward the kittens, Murray began to wonder how things would have turned out if children had come on the scene.

Luna dominated the people in her life, and she called the shots with Wily, too. "She plays it both ways," said Lois. When Lois was around, Luna was extremely personable, almost dog-like in her devotion; she'd follow her Person from one room to the next, perching on her shoulder, wriggling under the covers in bed, and keeping close watch near the tub while Lois bathed. When Lois was away or asleep, the kittens turned into desper-ados.

For months Wily remained backstage when people were around. When she did start coming out more frequently, Lois and Murray would shower her with attention to reward her bravery. But Luna didn't like sharing the limelight; she'd immediately crowd in on any interaction and try to steal back the show. If Murray managed to get shy Wily to play with a feather on a small fishing pole, "fishing for kittens" as he called it, Luna would want to get in on the game, and she'd soon take it over. She also claimed control at mealtime, nosing into and eating from both bowls before she'd let Wily begin dinner.

For the most part, the good natured Wily put up with her scene-stealing sister, recognizing Luna's natural authority and loving her companionship. One evening, however, when Lois and I had been playing actively with Luna in the living room, it turned out that Wily, ignored and off by herself in the bedroom, was taking out her frustration by quietly gnawing through an expensive cashmere sweater Lois had left on her bed.

The two cats became increasingly rambunctious, inseparable partners in crime. Once Lois left town for six days, leaving the cats in the care of a neighbor who, though he came in to feed them every day, didn't spend any time interacting with the pair. When Lois returned, the apartment appeared to have been ransacked: kitty litter had been tracked through the tiny apartment, the place was festooned with toilet paper and paper towels, plants were overturned, the bedspread had been pulled off the bed, and the sheet was torn off the couch. It was as if Dr. Seuss's Cat in the Hat had paid a visit, but hadn't cleaned up by the time Mother got home.

Certain aspects of having two cats in a small apartment started to annoy Murray. He complained that since the cats arrived, he could not get a good night's sleep at Lois's place. After the humans retired, the pair would launch into what he called "the kitty Olympics." Luna would leap from the windowsill to the bed, he told me, then tear across the bed, fly through the hall, and crash into the living room. Wily would take a parallel route, but she'd race under the bed instead of over it, and then they'd lock together in a loud wrestling match in the hallway. Resounding thumps suggesting that considerable damage was being done would punctuate the night, but in the morning, curiously, everything was intact.

Lois and Murray's previous cat, Lushka, who had died years earlier, had been quiet and delicate. When she joined people in bed, she would step gingerly around them, sniffing tentatively as she carefully raised each paw in the air before placing it down gently. In contrast, Luna would step directly on anything or anyone in her path: limbs, heads, neck, or hair. She seemed oblivious to the fact that sleeping humans were sentient beings. And unlike Lushka, who would get out of the way the moment she sensed someone needed to turn over, Luna was difficult to dislodge from a particular spot. One night, half-asleep, Lois saw Murray kick Luna off the bed. When she confronted him about it in the morning, he swore he was simply lifting the cat with his foot, an action he had been forced to take simply to turn over.

Murray tried patiently (and, increasingly, somewhat desperately) to tire the cats out thoroughly before bedtime with elaborate toys suspended from bamboo rods. He'd circle a dangling, feathered bird tantalizingly in front of Luna, until, her resistance broken, she started doing laps from the hall to the far end of the tiny living room, round and round in pursuit of the toy, until she had to lie down panting in the hall. He'd toss a fluffy ball down the hallway, over and over, and she'd fetch it like a dog.

One evening while Lois was drawing a bath, Luna, always a bit on the clumsy side, fell into the water while walking on the narrow, curved ledge. In a flash, she leapt out of the hot liquid and dashed to the safety of the living room. When Lois came out to make sure Luna was okay, Wily was licking the water off her fur and shielding her body. Wily looked at Lois fiercely. "What have you done to my sister?" her usually gentle eyes seemed to ask.

By the time Luna was nine months old, it was becoming clear that something was very wrong. Occasionally she would become first clingy, then crabby. Her breathing would grow faster and her pupils dilate. Her usually voracious appetite would disappear, her food would go untouched. Instead of following Lois from room to room, she would hide away in the closet or under the bed. During one such spell I lifted up the futon mattress to look at her through the bed-frame slits, and the usually friendly kitten hissed and lashed out at me like a viper.

We began to notice a pattern emerge. Every ten days to two weeks, Luna would get sick. Often she'd be out of sorts one evening and much worse in the morning, but significantly improved when Lois returned from work. By the time Lois could get her to the vet's, the symptoms had usually disappeared, although her heart rate would still be rapid with a faint murmur underneath. Asthma was the first diagnosis. We were all relieved by the ordinariness of the ailment. Surely something so common could be managed.

A steroid was prescribed. Lois got rid of her incense, cleaned out her closet, and bought a dust-free litter formula. She pored through cat books, consulted with the owners of the holistic pet food store, bought premium, additive-free cat food, and supplemented Luna's diet with vitamins and herbs said to be good for asthma. She added homeopathic remedies. Nothing seemed to help. Luna continued to have spells regularly. But it was hard to correlate her attacks with anything: it didn't seem to be the weather, the dust in the air, or what she ate. And in spite of everyone's best efforts, she seemed to be getting worse. Sometimes she would get so feverish that tiny beads of sweat would collect on her soft, black paws. Murray fretted over the poor condition of her whiskers. He noticed they seemed sparse and irregular, especially when compared to the long, bushy set on the cheeks of another cat we knew.

Overwhelmed at work, stressed out, and feeling confined in her small apartment, Lois needed a break, but with her cat getting sick so often, she had a hard time getting away. One Thursday night just as Lois and Murray had finally arranged to leave for a weekend at a seaside hotel in Montauk, Luna suffered another bad episode. Her temperature was high, her blood chemistry was out of whack, and the vet was very alarmed, so Lois boarded her for care and observation. After a day and a half the doctor left a message for Lois. Her kitty still had a fever, her eyes were still dilated, and she wasn't responding the way the vet had expected. "This is beyond my level of expertise," said the vet. "It doesn't seem to be asthma, and she isn't responding to antibiotics. I recommend you take her to a neurologist."

Since Lois was away, I picked Luna up. When I arrived, she seemed almost her normal self: alert, restless, tongue poking out just a bit. When I held her, she pushed hard against my chest with her hind legs, pulling out the threads in my sweater, and slipped out of my arms to further investigate the room that she had only viewed from inside her cage. She wanted to look at everything. She peered at each of the other cats in their respective cages, she sniffed at the stainless steel examining station, she went back to the cats, she wanted to be held again, and then she wanted to get away. Although I was prepared to take her back home, the doctor suggested I get her to the emergency room of the Animal Medical Center immediately.

Between long telephone conferences with Lois in her beachside room, I spent that Saturday night sitting in the emergency room, along with a woman whose dog had swallowed a battery, a girl who was bottle-feeding a two-day-old kitten, another girl who had found a cat beneath a truck that seemed to be paralyzed with a broken pelvis, and a teenager with a sick iguana. After a wait that seemed disproportionately long, consid-

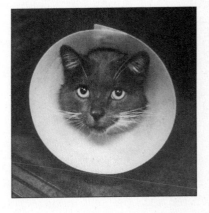

ering how few people were there, Luna was examined. Blood was taken. Her bile acids were checked. Five hours and $225 later we left with an appointment for the following day. Luna needed a second, more thorough bile acid test, but she had to be fasting when she came in.

That second test implicated Luna's liver in whatever was going on. It seemed likely that she had a shunt, a structural deviation from the normal passage of blood in and out of the liver. Lois was told to put her on low-protein food, which cats don't like. She also had one medicine to give Luna in the morning and another to give her at night. One of these, a Phenobarbital derivative to keep Luna from going into seizures when the acids built up in her brain, had an intensely bitter taste, and Lois had to devise elaborate schemes to get a precise quantity down her throat. The most successful method was to mix it with a little squash and rice baby food. But this mixture couldn't just be left out for Luna, because Wily might eat it. So Lois started feeding Luna first, up on the countertop. Wily would look up, a hurt, angst-ridden expression on her face. "Why does Luna get special treatment?" her eyes seemed to ask.

Soon the taste of the baby food wasn't enough to get Luna's medicine down, it had to be presented to Luna on a teaspoon or a finger so she could lick it off with her rough, pink tongue. Lois began to feel like a prisoner. There was no one, except for me, whom she could trust with the complicated protocol of feeding and medication. And I didn't want to stick around every weekend, either.

Even with the new medicines and the low-protein food, Luna's episodes continued. Lois couldn't stand to see her in so much pain, with her fevers, her migraines, and her loss of coordination and bladder control. Some mornings Luna seemed so sick that Lois was afraid she'd come home and find her dead. But quite often when she returned home the episode was over, and Luna would be back to her old curious, trusting, ready-to-play self, seeming to harbor no memories of her pain.

The medicine wasn't really working, even when the vet increased the dosage. Something had to be done, and Lois didn't think she could take Luna—who, when she wasn't having seizures, was lively, funny, and devoted—in for euthanasia.

Surgery seemed to be the only option, and there were no guarantees that it would work, either. The diagnosis wasn't straightforward—no shunt had shown up on the CAT scan, but it couldn't be completely ruled out.

The idea of surgery, with its price tag of $1,500 to $3,000, had taken some getting used to. In my prerescue years of cat owning, I had never spent more than a hundred dollars here and there on veterinary bills. Lois worked for a United Nations agency, on behalf of people whose average per capita income was less than a dollar a day. "It seems almost obscene, doesn't it?" commented Murray, who darned his own socks and who had been raised, along with his brother, in a one-bedroom apartment where a dresser drawer served as his crib.

It seemed like a lot of money to all of us. Lois complained about the expense, but felt she had to do everything she could for little Luna, and in this day of sophisticated veterinary medical technology, that means quite a lot. "Well, what's money for?" she asked, if not to save her spirited, wise-beyond-her-age little kitty.

Worse than the money issue was the possibility of an unforeseen problem that might mean a protracted recovery, with Luna stuck in a steel cage at the animal hospital, sick and alone. That was the worst-case scenario. We decided the best plan would be to have the doctors open her up to see if she looked operable. If her situation looked dubious or complicated, they were not to wake her up. Lois told the surgeon it was Luna's quality of life, not her life at any cost, that she was trying to save.

So one Thursday morning at seven, Lois took Luna in for surgery. The hospital waiting room was filled with tearful pet owners, all of whom were placing their animals into the hands of the surgical teams.

It wasn't easy. Luna had been especially spunky that week. For the first time, she had wanted to go outside Lois's apartment to investigate the hallway. On the cab ride to the hospital, she repeatedly slipped out of her box and tried to hide under the seat, as if to escape her fate.

"No need to hang around," the brilliant, overworked, gruff surgeon told Lois.

So Lois went home to a long, sad day of working at home and waiting by the phone.

Shortly after noon, the doctor called. Luna's condition was worse than dubious; it was, for all practical purposes, inoperable. Her liver had not just one but a spiderweb of shunts blocking the normal flow of blood into and out of the organ. The surgeons had never seen anything like it in a cat. They were not going to wake her up. They had no facilities for cremation. She was just gone—everything but her scent, which lingered under the bed and in her carrier.

"How's Wily doing?" I asked Lois when we went out to dinner later that day. Wily, by this time, was accustomed to Luna disappearing for a day or two.

"She knows," said Lois. Around half past one, at about the time Luna would have been breathing her last, Wily had made a rare daytime appearance. "She came out of the closet into the kitchen with a strange expression," said Lois. "She seemed really upset."

Lois was devastated that evening, but steely. She had been prepared. "I never got one good piece of news about that cat," she said.

I had remained optimistic as usual, thinking Luna would be likely to emerge from the surgery cured. When I heard she had died, I worried about Lois and Wily. I thought they would be the ones to grieve.

But the next day my whole torso ached and my heart felt tight. I wasn't expecting the visceral pangs of grief that accompany the death of a loved one.

It's just a little kitten, I said to myself. So many kittens in the world.

But I had never seen one quite like Luna, with her monkey face and her cocked head, suggesting a brilliant mind to go with her impetuous ways.

Better she should die than continue to suffer, I told myself. Better Lois gets on with her life. But still, my sides hurt.

The next day while Lois was still at work, I went over to her apartment. I wanted to sit shiva, more or less, with Wily. The apartment seemed so empty without Loonie there to greet me. Wily was hiding away in the closet. I cried silently, and then I cried aloud, partly because it seemed to ease the pain but also because I wanted Wily to hear my emotional distress. I wanted her to know that I felt the loss, too, that it wasn't only her. I felt that the sounds of grief must transcend the border between species.

A little later, after I had dried my tears and was sitting in the dark, I heard a faint, plaintive meow from the other room. It was the first peep I had heard from Wily since the time she had been alone in my bathroom. Lois was surprised, too, when I told her; she had never heard Wily vocalize. But after that, Wily started talking quite often.

A few days later a cab driver told me about how his father's ten cats in Bangladesh had started howling when his father died. "They were crying so loudly—just when he died. They never did that. How did they know he was dead?" the cab driver asked. "How did they know he wasn't just away?"

"I've lost lots of cats," said Richard, when I told him about Luna. "The best way to get over it is to get another one." I, too, thought it would be nice for Wily to have a little kitten to play with. It was kitten season; there was no shortage of animals needing homes. But Lois was not ready to take on another cat. This last one had been too much: too adorable, too exhausting, too expensive, and too heartbreaking. Lois also wanted to see if Wily would come around more quickly without a playmate. And slowly but surely she did.

Wily started to spend more time in the same room with people. She'd sit very near Lois and sometimes roll around seductively in front of her, exposing her vulnerable, tawny tummy. But if anyone made a move in her direction, she would dash off.

Even when Luna was alive, it was possible to sneak a few strokes across Wily's thick coat when she was cornered in the closet and hidden from view. But in the weeks after Luna was gone, she started to actually enjoy being petted when she was sitting in what became known as the "petting station," a knee-high shelf in the closet behind some dresses. One morning as Lois stroked her in the closet, she felt the distinctive vibration of purring. For a long time, the rule had been that you couldn't look at Wily. Looking spoiled everything. One glimpse of a human face and Wily would be gone, slipping away into another, less accessible corner of the closet, as if she couldn't tolerate the combination of visual and tactile human contact. If she didn't actually see a person, perhaps she could disassociate, she could pretend that she was rolling around with another cat. But there was no other cat; it was just her and us now.

One day while she was purring to my caresses, I parted the thick wad of clothes in Lois's overstuffed closet and came face-to-face with Wily. Her doe eyes, just a few inches away, returned my gaze. She remained still while I stroked her back near the tail, and she pushed up her backside up into my stroking. Her eyes stayed calm. She didn't look relaxed, exactly, but she wasn't running away. I blinked slowly at her a couple of times—a gesture that, in the cat world, is like throwing a kiss. She didn't respond with her eyes, so I let the clothes fall back down while I kept petting her. She rolled toward my hand, pushed her head against my fingers; it seemed she was asking for more pressure, more pleasure. Finally I had established visual and physical contact with this cat who had been so wild and so shy. I was reminded of a quote by Fernand Mery: "God created cats so that man could have the pleasure of caressing the tiger." ❧

Chapter 8

Cat People

Based on the responses of 177 participants in a survey conducted in Brooklyn, New York, it was ascertained that 22.0 per cent of the respondents fed free-ranging cats (2.8 per cent daily and 19.2 per cent occasionally) . . . Daily feeders were devoted to their cats. They continued to feed them despite the disapproval of their neighbors, financial constraint, or social obligations. Free-ranging cats appear to be in a mutually life-enhancing relationship with their feeders.

—Carol Haspel and Robert E. Calhoun,
"The Interdependence of Humans and
Free-Ranging Cats in Brooklyn, New York"

When Collette, a famed cat fancier, wrote that "One only risks becoming richer by associating with the cat," she must have been talking about sweet house kitties. Working with strays and feral cats, though arguably enriching, entails certain risks beyond bites, scratches, and fleas.

I have come to know several people who spend much—if not most—of their disposable income on cat food and veterinary bills. I've met some who have put their relationships, their housing, their free time, and their mental stability on the line for these beguiling creatures. I have seen an animal rescuer slip off into the murky territory of the "collector," a bona fide mental disorder well known to animal control officers and rescue groups, who are often called in to deal with the messes collectors leave behind. When apparently kindly eccentrics start taking in cats by the dozen without the resources to take care of them, the end is rarely pleasant. Most of the cat guardians I knew, however, while slightly quirky, were generally balanced, hardworking, and intelligent; they simply have a very soft spot for felines in trouble.

During my first year or two on the Lower East Side, cat people were as invisible to me as the cats they looked after. When I read, years ago, in the *New York Times* that an animal rescuer resided "on almost every block," I didn't think the article described my neighborhood. But now the figure seems about right to me. As I spent more time at the feeding station and looking for help, I became acquainted with a network of people caring for cats in various ways. Like the cats they watched over, these caretakers had their own informal, and sometimes overlapping, territories: Vera handled the blocks east and south of me to the East River. Carmen kept an eye on a few blocks north of and under the Williamsburg Bridge. Carol and Lee worked farther west. On the block directly west of my building, a feisty crone named Grace fed Blackie, a female whom I had trapped and had spayed. Though feral, Blackie would wait for Gracie to emerge from her entrance and trot alongside her as Grace slowly circumnavigated the block. For a week or two a man was coming by the feeding station in back of my apartment almost daily with a box of dry food. One day when I was out trying to trap one of Tammy's offspring, I asked him if he could hold off for a couple of days, so the kittens would get good and hungry. He tried to give me the box of food he had brought with him. "Oh, no, you take it home," I told him. He pushed the box back to me. "I don't have a home," he said.

I ran into Richard occasionally in the East Village. Sometimes in the afternoons, I'd find him headed toward a nearby cemetery where he fed pigeons and squirrels. I cringed when he first told me about this activity—it seemed almost foolhardy for someone so acutely sensitive to the suffering of animals to allow another species into his circle of compassion. In any case, it had not occurred to me that squirrels were in dire need of human assistance.

One day when I ran into Richard on his rounds, he invited me to hear his band play that evening at the Mercury Lounge on Houston Street. Watching him perform that evening for a small crowd and a crew that was taping the show for French television, I had trouble reconciling the cat trapper I knew with the guy on stage belting out lyrics of love and anger and loss. When trapping, Richard had an undeniable grace, but he also seemed somewhat frail and distracted. He was pale, almost painfully thin, and winced at sirens and other loud city noises. Before opening doors, he rolled his long shirtsleeves over his hands to avoid germs. "I try not to touch any public surfaces," he told me. "It's kind of a phobia of mine."

Onstage, though, with his long legs in tight jeans, his curly, dark hair falling toward his face, his satin shirt and his velvet vest, he looked like the quintessential British Invasion rocker. His pallor and his slenderness were perfect for the part. For one song's finale, he leapt acrobatically into the air with his guitar, and I wondered how he found time to stay in such good shape. His beautiful wife, Nancy, who played bass and sang backup, looked the part as well, slim and unsmiling with shoulder-length hair, dark eye makeup, a black shell, and shiny plastic jeans. Onstage, Richard looked like a guy whose life was rock and roll. Offstage, I knew him as a rescuer dedicated to the point of obsession—or saintliness, I wasn't sure which—to the homeless cats he came across so often.

Richard was always pleased to show off his brood. The first time I stopped by the apartment that he and Nancy shared with their cats, Richard was trying to coax Tiny, a cat with the proportions of a young seal, up and down a few stairs for a bit of a workout.

Three litter boxes were lined up along the entryway and a few others were strategically placed in other areas. A tower of plastic cat carriers and traps stood in a corner of the fairly small four-room apartment. Cats were lounging on almost every surface. One of the larger members of the household strained the sides of a lightweight cardboard box on the floor. A trio of newly arrived, still semi-feral tabbies perched on two carpeted cat trees in the middle room. Another cat peered down at us from a spot high atop a bookshelf. Two sprawled on the bed. A few walked around our ankles. Another time when I stopped by, twelve of the cats were spread out in regular intervals on Nancy and Richard's wide bed, suggesting a surrealistic quilt.

The place didn't exactly smell bad—Richard told me they found that a cedar-scented kitty litter did the best job of managing odors—but it was heavy with the presence of cats. Although I sometimes got annoyed with Casey for not being more gracious about the visitors that stayed with us on occasion, I was grateful that day for her selfishness. In a way she protected me, helping me to set boundaries, keeping my home and life from falling into chaos.

For years, Nancy and Richard had drawn the line at twelve cats. "When one dies, there's always someone waiting in the wings," Richard told me. But when three feral littermates had nowhere to go, they joined the family. And then a very sweet black cat showed up, literally left on their doorstep, and he stayed, too.

"We probably should have kept it at twelve cats," Richard mused one day. "But sixteen doesn't seem any worse in terms of the smell and cleaning up. It's just that with twelve, you could look around and once in awhile there'd be an empty chair or something. Now there's a cat wherever you look. Sometimes when I go to bed at night, I realize I haven't played with or talked to some of the cats. That's really unusual for me."

Richard and Nancy's cats seemed fairly ordinary to me—mostly tabby and tuxedo shorthairs, with one calico thrown into the mix. But in Richard's eyes, each was uniquely wonderful.

"He's *such* a sweetheart," Richard said when I marveled at Tiny's girth. "He was starving when we first found him."

"She's a *really* good cat," he said about Mommy Cat, whom he had brought in, pregnant, off the street. Nancy and Richard ended up keeping a few of her kittens, which had got their current brood off to a healthy start. Now, years later, they give Mommy Cat subcutaneous fluids morning and night to sustain her failing kidneys.

"He's a sweetie," he said about Monkey, the cat whose urinating on the television was the first symptom of a tumor requiring brain surgery. Like Colette, Richard believed that no cat is ordinary.

Richard seemed to happen upon cats in distress with alarming regularity. One afternoon I ran into him at the counter of an East Village health food store. "You wouldn't believe what happened yesterday," he said. As we walked out of the store he told me the story.

On their way home from brunch, he and Nancy had noticed a man walking across the street with a little kitten. Something struck Richard as odd—probably the way the man was holding the cat out stiffly away from his body—so he watched closely as the man disappeared behind a building, returning without the kitten. Richard investigated and found the three-month-old black kitten in a garbage can. After retrieving the kitten and taking him home, Richard returned to investigate. It turned out that the man's mother had an apartment full of cats—about twenty-five or thirty in all—and had been threatened with eviction in two days unless she got rid of the cats. Her son took matters into his own hands. A number of the cats had already been taken to the city animal shelter, where their survival chances were slim. Others had been dumped around the neighborhood.

Nancy and Richard convinced the man to let them into the apartment. Like so many other collectors' homes, it smelled terrible. The woman was old and professed to love cats, but her love, apparently, did not include neutering or vet care. She had started with one pair of cats and their kittens, and then more kittens were born, and before long she had an apartment caked in cat dust, feces, and urine, stinking and bug infested. "It's always the same at these collectors' apartments," said Richard. "To get to the cats, you have to get down on your hands and knees, and all this dirt and excrement gets all over your clothes and body. It's horrible." Richard's willingness to wallow in the filth seemed particularly heroic considering his phobia of germs.

Over the next few weeks, Richard removed the cats from the apartment, one or two at a time, and began the long process of finding homes for them. It was months before they were all placed; many found homes through Nancy's contacts on the Internet. In the meantime, the cats were boarded at a West Side veterinary hospital that served, essentially, as a holding pen. Nancy managed to get a $2,000 foundation grant for expenses, but still the rescue was grueling work.

Yet when he told me this story, Richard seemed to consider himself incredibly lucky that he had happened upon the man with the cat. "If we had come home a just few minutes later, we would have missed it," he said one day.

A couple of times when I started to tell Richard about the fate of some of Mimi's brood, he would stop me. "If it's a bad story about cats, don't tell me," he said. "I can't take hearing bad things about cats."

He never told me about the worst rescue he had worked on: I read about it in an interview he gave. He and some fellow trappers were called on to help in removing seventy cats from the apartment of one obviously disturbed collector. Refuse in the apartment was literally a couple of feet deep, and worse, over that was a layer of excrement. The cats were starving and caked in filth; they all appeared to be the same dirty shade of brown. Once the cats were out of the apartment—many were in such bad shape they had to be put to sleep—the collector's mother, dead three or four months, was discovered under the detritus.

I first met Vera on a drizzly Sunday evening when Richard and I were trying to trap Tammy and Seymour. As night fell, Vera came limping through the alley, pushing one of the tall, mesh, laundry and shopping carts that double as walkers for many of the neighborhood's older women. As Richard and I stood back to let the cats smell the bait, Vera, in an accent left over from her younger days in Berlin, asked whom we worked with. When I explained what we were doing, she removed a cloth from her shopping cart with a flourish, revealing two kitten traps. "I've trapped kittens for years here," she said. "I work with a partner who helps place the cats." We exchanged phone numbers, and she became my first ally who actually lived in the neighborhood.

The alley that bounded the little park where the cats lived wasn't on Vera's regular route because she had observed that the cats appeared to get enough food without her. Sometimes she came by when it rained, though, because she had noticed the cats seemed hungry on those nights. Vera, I later learned, taught German and Russian in the neighborhood, and acted as translator and scribe for members of the Russian community. Two days a week she took a bus to her philosophy class; other days she went to a community pool for a swim. Initially, seeing her in the dark, I thought she looked like any other nondescript older cat lady. But one summer day, I saw her fanning her face in the heat, and I realized that, with her angular jaw and her wide, round eyes, she must have been quite a beauty a few decades earlier, when her back was straighter and her face more taut.

Vera had seven "unadoptables," as she called them, at home. "I never planned to have so many," she told me. "But they weren't adoptable and I couldn't throw them out. What can I do?" One had only one eye; one had a heart murmur; she had taken in one of them, too old to place, when a friend died; one had poor toilet habits. And when other neighborhood kittens or cats needed temporary quarters, her hallway filled up with cages and carriers of foster cats. "When I had two cats, I used to go to Berlin for two weeks every year," she told me. "But with all these cats I can't go anywhere. I clean up after them for an hour in the morning, and it takes me an hour to feed them."

Vera estimated that she had taken in more than five hundred kittens from the neighborhood over the past few years, and that the woman who adopted them out, and who worked with other trappers as well, had found homes for nearly a thousand over the decade.

Every night around dusk, rain or shine, Vera would put her kitten traps and cat food in her little cart and start her route, walking slowly due to deteriorating cartilage in one hip. First she'd head up Henry Street to feed the cats in the courtyard

behind the school, then she'd walk over to the Drug Rehab Center near Gouverneur Hospital, where there was a population of twenty or more cats who came in and out through a basement window. Vera made a couple other stops along the way before finishing her rounds each night at the Fine Fair grocery store, where she'd pick up a few items before it closed at nine. One night I arranged to meet her at the store to borrow a kitten trap.

She had a strange "I told you so" look on her face. "See what I found," she said, pulling from her cart a half-eaten can of cat food liberally laced with green crystals.

"Rat poison?" I asked.

"I think so," she said, as she started to toss it into the corner trash can.

"Wait, don't throw that away," I said. "It's evidence."

Over the few months since I had met her, Vera had been talking about a bad situation across the street—cats living in a small, irregular-shaped open space in the middle of a triangular block. A few buildings with small, unkempt gardens or patios formed part of the border; a public school, a Torah center, and one of the Henry Street Settlement buildings also surrounded it. Natalie, a woman who lived in one of the houses that overlooked the courtyard had been feeding the cats, and she'd asked Vera to feed the cats when she left town for the winter. Vera didn't mind. She had been feeding and keeping the population down by trapping kittens there for years. But the situation had changed recently: One of the maintenance men at the school had begun to lock the gate that was Vera's access to the courtyard. And he hurled epithets at her and the cats through the fence.

Vera continued to leave food near the street, hoping the cats would find their way out to it, but she could no longer get into the courtyard to trap. Several times she told me she felt heart-broken about the situation. The group's numbers had swelled to twenty or so. Natalie hadn't given her a key for the basement, which would have given Vera access to the cats. She had said she would be back in May, and Vera waited anxiously for her return. But May passed with no word, then June came and went. Kitten season was in full swing in late July when Vera discovered the poison. Although the woman still had not returned, Vera finally got through to tell her what was going on, and she sent us keys so we could enter the courtyard.

For weeks Vera had been complaining that something "fishy" was going on in the courtyard. A number of the cats she had seen regularly were no longer coming out. One had looked at her with an expression of anguished pain, seeming barely able to walk. No wonder. The laboratory identified the green crystals as Brodifacoum, a poison used mainly for rats that works by blocking the blood's ability to clot. Cats who ingest it hemor-rhage internally over a period of a few days.

After getting the can of poisoned food from Vera, I called Richard. He had just finished rescuing the cats from the old lady's house, and was now taking care of four cats belonging to another old woman who had gone into a nursing home. Nevertheless, outraged by what he had heard, he was ready to spring into action on the spot, to run over right away with traps—it was about ten o'clock at night—and to keep watch to find out who had put out the poison. None of that seemed feasible, though, since at that time we lacked access to the interior courtyard. Even the area where Vera had found the poison was usually closed off by the locked gate.

"I can climb really high, if I need to," Richard said when I mentioned the fence.

It seemed unlikely that anything else would happen that night. So Richard gave me some numbers to call, the ASPCA police among others, while he mulled the situation over. When we spoke again an hour later, he and Nancy had devised a plan. She would make a sign using her computer at work, and we would post it all over the neighborhood, hoping to scare the culprit. The next morning she faxed me the sign in bold black lettering.

REWARD

In cooperation with the ASPCA police and the NYPD, we are offering a $200 reward for information leading to the arrest and conviction of the person or persons responsible for poisoning cats in this area. Poisoning cats is a punishable crime. The sentence is one-year imprisonment and a $1,000 fine.

I made copies and posted them around the block. In the meantime, Richard had talked to Dr. Cotter and learned that vitamin K, which helps blood coagulate, can be an antidote to rat poison. Richard got a prescription filled and headed over. Although Vera hadn't been able to get into the enclosed area for several months, Richard immediately started ringing doorbells and managed to talk his way in right away. Somehow, when Richard, with his unwavering commitment to save cats, got involved, things happened.

I wondered what we would do with these feral cats once we caught them, recalling that the last two feral cats Richard told me about ended up in an apartment with twenty-five others. Richard didn't seem concerned: They weren't safe where they were, so they had to be removed. Some might turn out to be tame.

I found Richard on the stoop in front of the basement, where he had gained access to the courtyard. He had already found two dead cats and snatched three tiny kittens that were sleeping in the sun by scruffing them up with his hands. The kittens were in a box ready to be taken to a veterinarian, and Richard was waiting to see if another cat would enter the trap. He was terrified that he might pick up a nursing mother and that the rest of her kittens, left alone, might die. On the other hand, if there was more poison out, a cat might die that way, too.

"I can't take this," he said under his breath. "This is a life and death situation. It's too much."

Nevertheless, he did take it. Almost every afternoon for weeks he called to discuss that day's plan. Day after day he took the bus down there and set traps. Sometimes he climbed over high Cyclone fences to get the traps into better positions or to see if he could grab any more kittens.

Once I helped him get traps to the other side of the court-yard. To get there, he had to climb a creaky wooden ladder and hoist himself over a Cyclone fence covered with barbed wire, which he first had to cut and cover with old towels to avoid hurting himself. Once over the fence, he balanced himself on the wooden crossbeam of a shaky old pergola, and dangled his foot to get a toehold on the other side of the Cyclone fence. Then he jumped a few feet down to a chair placed on the other side of the fence. Meanwhile, I stood on the ladder, handing him empty traps and taking them back when we got a cat. "Don't try to do this on your own," he warned me sharply more than once; the idea of attempting it hadn't even occurred to me.

The courtyard rescue continued for months. In the meantime, other cat emergencies popped up with regularity. One evening in the aftermath of the poisoning, Richard discovered, on his way home, a beautiful calico cat impaled on an iron fence. Because there was a towel nearby, Richard suspected that the cat had been thrown from the roof or window of an apartment building nearby. Shaken, he bundled up the dead cat and brought it to a nearby vet's office for proper disposal. But that wasn't the end of it: "Every night," he told me days later, "I'll be in the middle of a regular dream, and then I'll see the image of the cat on the fence and wake up."

Two days after finding the dead calico, Richard found a young, friendly, all-black cat at the doorway as he was leaving his apartment. Since it didn't seem to belong to anyone on the block, he put it in his bathroom overnight and took it to the vet in the morning.

"Did you think about putting up signs in the neighborhood in case someone had lost it?" I asked.

"Oh, I wouldn't do that," Richard said. "First of all, if they let the cat get out into the street, it's probably not a safe home. And if it belonged to someone who wanted the cat, they would have put signs all over the neighborhood."

During that same period, Vera brought the plight of Robin to my attention, after the cat, which was obviously not used to the out-of-doors, had perched for two days on an upper branch of a magnolia tree in a small park near the East River. The park rangers had gotten him down once, but then, terrified by the wholly unfamiliar environs, he scurried even higher up the tree after an unsuccessful attempt to climb a steel lamppost. When he had been in the tree for four days, barely moving, we persuaded the fire department to come.

The firemen blazed up to the park, surveyed the situation, and pulled a twenty-foot aluminum ladder from the fire truck. When it was balanced precariously against the tree's slim trunk and limbs, one of the fireman dashed up as if it were a wide staircase. "I've been on the force eighteen years, and this is the first time we've gone after a cat," said one of the firemen, after I complimented him on the crew's approach to public service. When I got Robin to the vet, we found he had already been neutered and his neck still bore the imprint of where a collar had been.

By the middle of September, after devoting much of the summer to the project in the courtyard across the street, Richard, Vera, and I completed our first "trap-neuter-return"

program, the method of cat management advocated by Alley Cat Allies and other groups around the country. We had captured all but one of the adult cats that were being poisoned in the courtyard across the way. Since the remaining female was fertile, we realized that the population might spike upward again, but we simply weren't able to get her. These cats were clearly feral and showed no signs of welcoming socialization. We gave up trying to place them since the market was flooded—even adorable kittens and friendly, declawed, and pedigreed cats were not finding homes easily that summer—and two of the cats seemed aggressive. We did manage to adopt out seven of the eight kittens. The eighth, who had already lost an eye to a herpes infection, died in the car as Richard rushed him to the vet. We had worked with the Humane Society's law enforcement officer and school officials to make sure the poisoning would not reoccur. And with the cooperation of an animal-loving facilities manager, we made arrangements to come through a building into the courtyard twice a week to leave food and water in large plastic dispensers. It turned out to be our first managed colony.

We took five of the adult cats, all of whom looked thin, weak, and dull after being caged at the vet's all summer, and released them back into their home area. At first they seemed paralyzed, unable to leave their carriers. After a few minutes we turned the carriers slightly on end and tapped on the back. Four of the cats shot out and bolted under the chain-link fence into the inner courtyard. The fifth tried to go straight up a brick wall over the basement stairs. She climbed perhaps thirty feet on toeholds invisible to us, and then, scared, with nothing to hold on to and no safe ledges, she fell back down into the stairwell. We left then, so as not to add to her panic and to give her a chance to find another exit route. After that we only caught glimpses of the cats on our feeding rounds, but from neighbors' reports, the little band was doing okay. The project, which was supported by another $2,000 of grant money that Richard's wife procured and by some of our own contributions, had at least stabilized the population.

I felt somewhat discouraged. Despite all that money and all that work—weeks and weeks of trapping and transporting cats, and making endless calls to figure out what to do with them—we had only made a dent in the growth of one colony. One tiny dent in a national population of feral cats that is reported to be as high as sixty million—roughly equivalent to the number of owned cats. But later, after I had gotten another colony under control and talked to other people who were doing the same work, I grew more optimistic. I began to think that we were on the verge of a paradigm shift—not only in terms of feral cats but, in a more general sense, about how we perceive animals and their right to exist. 🐾

— Chapter 9 —

Pretty Casey

As we own cats by human rules of ownership, so cats own us by cat rules of ownership. As a wild cat owns a territory and the rights to hunt the mice or the deer thereon, so a housecat owns a human dwelling and the rights to the people.

—*Elizabeth Marshall Thomas,*
Tribe of the Tiger

"Do cats understand the concept of work?" I asked Gail before leaving on a ten-day business trip. Casey was not in good shape—by this point she needed subcutaneous fluids each day because of her failing kidneys—and I hated leaving her alone for such a long time. I'd contacted Gail so I could tell Casey that she'd be taken care of by others in my absence, and that being away so long was not my idea.

"They understand that you have a purpose outside the house," Gail told me. "I'll tell Casey that you have to go away because of your purpose in life. She understands that."

Not only do pets understand the concept of purpose, they thrive when they feel that they are fulfilling a particular role in a household, according to Penelope Smith. Smith is Gail's mentor in animal communications and author of the book *Animal Talk*.

Some animals see themselves as protectors, some as clowns, Smith writes. She tells of a turtle that simply sought to radiate warmth and cheerfulness to the household and of a cat whose purpose was to see her owner attain spiritual growth. Casey's function, it seemed clear from her sensuous movements and her way of positioning herself to best advantage, was to bestow beauty and grace on my life. It also seemed that she could teach me a thing or two about feminine power while she was at it. In the process of helping me out in those ways, she had an item on her personal agenda as well: to establish property rights over both her territory and her Person.

Whenever I tried to introduce her to new cats or kittens who needed homes, Casey would become in turn, angry, aggressive, cold, withdrawn, and finally, sick. As she grew older and started to have health problems, I tried to limit fostering to a week or two at time and, even then, only in the most desperate situations. And I made sure these temporary foster cats stayed in the bathroom. Casey didn't seem to mind sharing the apartment with an untouchable feral kitty or two, as long as they stayed out of sight. However, once she noticed a bond forming between me and another cat, any time she sensed an emotional pull, she started to get upset.

"Of course she gets upset," said my vet, who seemed to understand cat psychology. "They're not supposed to be in her place."

That was exactly how Casey assessed the situation. When I saw that the stream of visiting felines was making her depressed, I talked to her about the situation, with Gail translating.

Gail explained to Casey that the foster cats stayed temporarily, only because they had nowhere else to go. "But this is my home," Casey protested.

"Of course it's your home," Gail said to soothe her. She described the plight of the homeless outdoor cats who needed help, but Casey did not seem overly concerned about their well-being.

With her usual tact, Gail had started the conversation with a compliment. "When I ask your Person to describe you," she told Casey, "she always says how beautiful you are."

"That's because I am," my furry diva replied.

I thought Casey was gorgeous from the moment I first glimpsed her in a narrow hallway at the top of a stairway. I always think of her as being blue-gray, the color of shadows. But sometimes, with the pink of her skin and blood vessels showing through on her ears and forehead, there's a hint of mauve as well. In the light she gleams like burnished metal. Sleek and exquisitely proportioned, with a fluffy coat and a small, expressive face, Casey often reminds me of the Burmese or Russian blues I see in cat books. Her father's Siamese blood-lines are revealed in both her elegant lines and her ability to speak up loudly when she has a serious complaint. She's either extremely intelligent or somewhat telepathic, or, more prob-ably, both. And she's a prima donna: unafraid to make her pref-erences clear, quick to signal displeasure, capable of giving me the cold shoulder for days if some aspect of her care is less than satisfactory.

When I serve Casey food that she deems objectionable—which could even be a flavor that she seemed to relish a few days earlier—she'll take one whiff of it and run off to another room, as if deeply offended. If the food is only mildly objec-tionable, she'll sniff warily and then back away from it very slowly. On the other hand, if she catches the aroma of some-thing she likes, she'll sit waiting by her bowl, all alert and expec-tant, with her front legs held very straight beneath her, her chest puffed out a bit, and her eyes soft and wide. How could I not try hard to please her?

During the day, Casey does not dole out—or readily accept—much affection. She lets me know, however, that she appreciates a couple of good, stiff brushing sessions during the day, after which she runs across the room and rakes her claws across the carpet. But at night, after I turn out the light and when I'm just on the verge of sleep, she turns amorous. She curls into my arms purring loudly, cozies into little nooks and crannies formed by my body, or settles directly on my chest or hip. She tends to wake me up in the morning by staring into my face or meowing loudly just before the alarm clock rings.

When friends visit, she usually runs and hides. If she deigns to stay in view and someone tries to pet her, she'll swipe lightly or simply raise one paw straight up in an imperial gesture of warning. She reserves her affection solely for me. I don't know what it is about me that pleases her so. Maybe that first day when she found me in the hallway, she intuited that I would be an obedient servant, eminently trainable.

Several years ago, after finally getting an apartment that allowed pets, I began talking about getting a cat. But three or four months passed and I was still catless. My boyfriend at the time used this to berate me: I was ineffectual, unable to act decisively. I explained carefully to him more than once that I didn't want to simply go out and look for a cat. In my experience, the perfect cats have always somehow managed to find me: Adorable Nepenthe, a tiny ball of blue-gray fur with matching eyes, summoned me on a street corner in San Francisco; darling Nanook was dropped off at my house by a friend; pregnant Smokey showed up at my doorstep. My boyfriend, Tad, acted like I was just making excuses. But soon thereafter Casey found me. And she's outlasted Tad by many years.

On that spring day I returned home much earlier than usual because I had been on jury duty. Walking up to my apartment, I heard loud meowing in the hall and responded, "Here, kitty, kitty." I was immediately smitten by the graceful creature that rounded the corner, looking so much like my long-lost Nepenthe. Casey practically leapt into my arms. (At least that's how I remember it. Quite possibly, I bent down and swooped her up. But certainly she was quite willing to allow herself to be picked up, quite uncharacteristically, as I later discovered.)

When I opened the door to my apartment, Casey walked right in and proceeded to investigate. I opened a can of tuna to make her feel at home, then fished in my closet for a litter box left over from when I took care of my sister's cat. I took a bath while this new arrival surveyed the apartment—sizing it up for possible future use, I later surmised. After a couple of hours enjoying a feline presence in the apartment, I realized that someone might be missing her, and put up a sign in the hall.

Soon afterward an adorable couple rang my bell. It was Tara, the rock guitarist/librarian and her tall boyfriend, Tim, also a musician, whom I recognized as the guy who had been kind enough and strong enough to help me carry furniture up the stairs a few months earlier. "Is Casey there?" they asked, and I invited them in.

It turned out that while vacuuming, Tim had left the door open for a few minutes and hadn't realized that Casey had ventured out. They lived in an apartment with the same floor plan two stories directly above me, which, perhaps, accounted for Casey's willingness to enter my place; it must have seemed somewhat familiar. Tim and Tara were obviously devoted to Casey. (Ten years later, Tara fished out of her wallet a faded photograph of Casey she always carried around, with a single white whisker taped to the back.) Tara had witnessed Casey's birth in Kentucky and picked her out of the litter expressly because of her sense of self-sufficiency. Even then Casey didn't like other cats much. When she was six months old, this Kentucky Cat, KC, was brought to New York.

"Well, if you ever need someone to look after her, let me know," I said as I surrendered Casey back to her owners.

A few months later, when Tim and Tara left town for a music tour, Casey stayed with the woman who was apartment-sitting for them. But the two never bonded, and when Tim and Tara

returned, the place was full of dander, which cats produce in greater quantities when they are under stress and which also produces an allergic reaction in many people.

Tim, always somewhat allergic to cats, reacted so violently to the dander that he was rushed to the emergency room, gasping for breath. With the help of an inhaler he had managed with his allergy for seven years, but after this episode the doctors insisted that the cat must go. Tara telephoned me, sobbing as she explained what had happened. Would I take Casey? Yes, I said without hesitation.

Tara came downstairs a few hours later, still crying and unable to speak as she handed Casey over to me. She returned an hour later, eyes now red and puffy, with Casey's feeding dishes and a gray stuffed rabbit that Casey liked to knead. That night when I went to sleep, Casey jumped on the bed and pushed her face into the pulse point in my neck, purring. From our first night together, Casey seemed to feel she belonged with me. I sometimes think that with feline prescience she had known she would soon need to find another home, and another human to do her bidding. She had succeeded admirably.

Initially, I hoped that some day Casey would take a fancy to one or another of the foundlings I brought home. I thought another cat would give her some stimulation or, at least, company when I was gone. Not incidentally, it would assuage my guilt at leaving her alone when I traveled. But Casey was not about to relinquish an inch of territory or to allow her Person—her meal ticket, her benefactor, her sole provider, her sleeping partner—to dilute her affections. Every time I brought in a new cat, I made an effort to shower Casey with extra attention, to assure her of her unassailable pre-eminence in my heart. Of course it was not easy to resist the charms of the newcomers.

Two shy, sweet collector's cats, Macavity and Posie, were so submissive to Casey that I thought she might get a kick out of having them to boss around, instead of just me. They came from the old woman who had twenty-three other cats and an eviction notice. Three-month-old, midnight-black Macavity had been pulled out of a garbage can. Macavity's older sister from an earlier litter, Posie, nearly escaped under a Cyclone fence, but Richard grabbed on to her tail and forcibly pulled her back out.

With her lopsided dots and splotches, Posie would have been described as piebald if she were a horse. Two black patches masked her eyes and one spilled around her mouth. When she moved through the house she traveled cautiously, hugging the walls and staying clear of open areas, an instinctual precaution, I speculated, designed to help cats maneuver around open fields without getting swooped up by an owl or hawk. In my apartment, though, she had only Casey to worry about.

Casey didn't seem to mind the pair for the first week or two, when they were locked out of sight in the bathroom. Of course she knew something was amiss and cast the occasional questioning look at me. But she did not seem especially anxious to learn more about what transpired behind the closed bathroom door. She'd hurry past it, as if to ignore the unpleasantness within. "It's just for a couple of weeks," I told Casey, and that's what I thought. Bide-A-Wee, a local no-kill shelter with a good reputation, had told me they would take Macavity and Posie. But each time I called, they'd push the date further into the future. In the meantime, I attempted to ratchet my diva-treatment of Casey up a notch higher.

I couldn't keep the new cats in the bathroom for more than about ten days. This was partly out of sympathy—it was so clear that they felt caged in the small, hot room—and partly that I physically couldn't manage it because of the way Posie raced to get past my legs to a safe hiding spot whenever I so much as cracked open the door.

None of the feral cats I had taken in earlier had displayed such behavior. While the really wild cats had remained crouched in a corner, afraid to venture into the rest of the house, Posie and Macavity, though shy, were basically socialized, domestic cats, responsive to handling and comfortable in a human environment. Nevertheless, once sprung from the bathroom, they cautiously squeezed themselves into the narrow space under my sofa for most of the day. Casey could ignore them there, too.

But after a couple of weeks, the space under the sofa must have become stuffy and boring, and my two guests began to hang out in the living room proper, watching me work. Casey, meanwhile, sequestered herself in my bedroom most of the day. Once in the morning and again at night, she would emerge, hostile, and tear out after one or the other of the new cats, forcing Posie back under the couch or cornering Macavity, who would adopt a submissive posture while Casey held him at bay, hissing with hair on end, until I intervened.

"No, Casey!" I would yell loudly, and Casey would look confused and angry. Then I would feel guilty. She was, after all, defending her territory—our territory—against what she perceived as intruders. And no one actually got hurt. After each skirmish Casey would climb, victorious, to the top of the sofa and scratch it vigorously. Before Posie and Macavity took up residence, I would have admonished her for such behavior. But now, I thought, she needed the assurance that, yes, this was still her living room, and yes, she alone could lay claim to the couch. In any case, cushions obscured the shoulder of the couch where she preferred to scratch.

This status quo remained in effect for a couple of months. Things, however, got worse when little Aaron came. He was the last of the seven kittens we caught from the tribe that was being poisoned in the courtyard across the way. I had agreed to take him in for just one night.

"Do you think you could hold on to him for a little longer?" Richard asked the next day. "We're just overwhelmed here." He and Nancy were up to sixteen cats by that time. They were in the midst of cleaning every surface in their bathroom, trying to remove any traces of fleas from the stray they had taken in overnight because the vet's office was closed. Even though I thought it was important to draw boundaries, their situation was so much more extreme than mine that I could hardly refuse.

Aaron was sick when he arrived, but the real trouble started when he started feeling better. He wanted out of the bathroom, and he wanted to play. He was fearless. At first Posie and Macavity wanted nothing to do with the young newcomer, but, undaunted, he kept trying to get their attention. He'd approach them in a Halloween-cat stance—back all arched, body held sideways, hair up on end—that made him look twice his normal size as he sidled toward them, lunging quickly, then jumping straight up into the air and landing on all fours before dashing away. Eventually they couldn't resist his invitations to play. Soon there were cats sprinting across the living room and sliding across the floors, waging mock battles, playing hide-and-seek, chasing each other's tails, and jumping up on chairs to ambush one another from above. These whirring, furry balls of energy were rather distracting as I attempted to plug away at my computer, and sometimes they had me laughing out loud. But I couldn't enjoy them wholeheartedly, not with Casey sulking, dejected, in my bedroom.

Like the child in the story "The Emperor's New Clothes," Aaron was too young and rambunctious to realize that he should display absolute deference to the regent of the territory. His youthful brazenness changed the power dynamics. Now there were three of "them" in the house, and Macavity had grown bigger and stronger. Inspired by the scrappy young Aaron, he suddenly seemed to realize that he need no longer kowtow to Casey. Obviously outnumbered and seemingly overwhelmed by the vortex of youthful feline energy in the apartment, Casey retreated to my bedroom as if under siege.

Her withdrawal hurt me because it was so out of character. Before this, Casey, even at the age of sixteen, had been so sure of her territorial rights that she was willing to take on Seymour, the big, much younger, former street-fighting tom. I redoubled my efforts to find homes for the other cats. But in the end it was Richard's wife who found a new Person for Macavity and Posie, and we brought Aaron along as a bonus.

When I returned after delivering the cats to their new home, my own Casey-kitty peered down on me from the top shelf of my closet. Her eyes were wide, tinged with the look of anguish—and, perhaps, betrayal—that she'd been wearing for weeks now. "It's okay, Casey," I said. "You have the run of the house again. Those other bad kitties are gone."

I cleaned the litter box the three guest cats had used, and vacuumed and mopped the floors. Then I carried Casey around the apartment, since she wouldn't go on her own. But with their combined scents still in the air, the other cats' presence lingered. It was a couple of days before Casey began tentative reconnaissance missions into the other rooms of the apartment and more than a week before she seemed to truly inhabit it.

Slowly she felt her way into the other rooms, resuming her favorite positions that were dictated by the slant of the sun and her passing whims: one moment hidden in the closet, the next stretched out on the back of the couch, then peering out a window, now lounging about on the rug waiting to be brushed. "What a cute kitty," I kept hearing myself cooing. "What a pretty kitty." Having Casey at ease in her house again, I felt as if I had placated its guardian spirit.

Sometimes when I glance over at my little gray Casey, all rolled into a ball, I think of my friend Chip. "Can you imagine how amazed someone from another planet would be by the concept of cats?" he once asked. "Don't you think they would marvel that these beautiful otherworldly beings consent to grace us with their presence?"

Actually, these beings made a rather practical bargain some five thousand years ago or so, when they insinuated themselves into the domestic sphere, trading in their rodent-catching abilities for regular meals, shelter, and care. Their domestication was late in the overall scheme of things—dogs, for instance, have been palling around with humans for some fourteen thousand years. This relatively recent domestication contributes to cats' ability to "go wild" rather quickly, although, like other domestic animals, the species has undergone a reduction in brain size compared to their wild ancestors, which is one of the reasons that even feral cats are somewhat dependent on humans. The Egyptians, who are thought to have domesticated cats, revered them. The early historian Herodotus relates that owners went into mourning and shaved their eyebrows when a cat died and that they mummified their cats and buried them in consecrated places. Today cats mainly barter their ability to offer beauty, companionship, and affection in return for food and shelter. And many, like Casey, have become extremely adept at getting their own way.

"Sounds like she's got you pretty well trained," my vet said to me one day, after I explained Casey's particular eating preferences to him. He didn't know the half of it.

He didn't know how she had trained me to pick a particular species of grass that grew in just a few spots near my apartment, and to feed it to her blade by blade. He couldn't have known that she had gradually communicated that her preferred way of drinking water was out of my cupped hands, fresh from the bathtub tap, preferably lukewarm. I was never sure whether the natural salts from my skin actually made it taste better or whether she just enjoyed turning me into her drinking bowl.

While watching a PBS *Nature* program about a man who trained cats to jump through hoops and perform other tricks, I realized that Casey had patiently employed exactly the same step-by-step techniques to train me. She rewarded me with expressions of pleasure when I was on the right track and dashed away with a look of reproach when I misunderstood. And who knows how many other techniques cats have at their disposal? A quote I saw on the Internet, attributed to Lilian Jackson Braun, had a certain resonance: "At dinner time he would sit in a corner, concentrating, and suddenly they would say, 'Time to feed the cat,' as if it were their own idea."

As I write, I look over and I see Casey stretched out in the sun, an elegant, living, breathing household adornment. Sometimes I feel that my only appropriate response is adoration, like that performed by the Egyptians depicted on the cases of cat mummies, their arms raised in postures of devotion. Sometimes I wonder whether the regal Casey was an Egyptian temple cat in a previous life. And I wonder whether in that life, too, I was her devoted servant. 🐾

— Chapter 10 —

Seymour's Last Stand

When your local 'amateur' says no, chances are no one else will say yes. There's almost nowhere to refer people for either rescue or placement. Adoption institutions always have long waiting lists to accept even the most adoptable animals, and New York City's 'Animal Rescue' delivers all rescuees to the Center for Animal Care and Control, where most are destroyed. Knowing there's no alternative places enormous pressure on volunteer animal workers like us who have ordinary jobs, modest incomes, no shelter, no office, no staff vets, no staff at all. It's hard not to add 'just one more' animal to the load, because we know that with hard work miracles can happen.

—City Critters Newsletter, *"Kitten Season"*

It wasn't Seymour's fault.

It was my fault for not changing the litter. My fault for not making sure the bathroom door was secured. My fault for bringing him over to my sister's, while she was away for a few weeks at her new house in the Berkshires, without asking her first.

I figured it wouldn't do any harm to have Seymour stay in the bathroom of Lois's apartment for just a few days until I could get him to the rest home in eastern Pennsylvania that had agreed to take him. I had meant to ask Lois first, but there was all this other stuff going on with my co-op board and her house closing and her new phone not working properly and all.

I meant to tell her, and then, after a couple of days, I figured it could wait until she got home and hadn't noticed a thing. But it *was* a brand new aqua Italian sofa that had been on order for months. Luna and Wily, whom she had taken off my hands, had shredded the last one. Why did Seymour have to go up there to relieve himself?

It was definitely my fault. I should have changed his litter, and then he wouldn't have felt the need to use the sofa. He had always used the litter box before.

I should have changed it. It *was* pretty wet. By this time Seymour's kidneys were failing, and I was administering 100 cc of fluids under his skin every day. He produced quite a volume of urine, although being mostly water, it hardly smelled. I was pressed for time or I definitely would have changed it.

When I entered the apartment the next morning, he was resting in his usual spot in the bathroom, but the door was ajar. And there on the sofa was his stool, like a rebuke. Seymour had tried to cover it with a towel.

Even though it wasn't Seymour's fault, I flipped out. After stripping the sofa cushions, rinsing the foam pillows, sniffing at everything, and looking for threads pulled out by scratching,

I packed Seymour up in the carrier. Even though he meowed plaintively and looked confused and alarmed, and even though the vet had said he shouldn't go back on the street, I hailed a cab and returned Seymour to the parking lot where I had picked him up a month or so earlier.

I felt like an addict, sneaking around guiltily and doing things I was reluctant to admit. I was afraid that cats were ruining my life. I was close to losing my apartment, and now I wondered if I might not lose my sister's trust as well. It was too much. Seymour would just have to go back to the parking lot until I could figure something out.

Most rescuers believe that friendly, socialized cats like Seymour belong indoors with people and that it's cruel to leave them on the streets. And since releasing Seymour back into the park a year or so earlier, I had continued to look for a home for him. But because of his FIV and his fighting with Casey, I hadn't meant to take him on board myself. In any case, he seemed happy enough outdoors. He was on good terms with Tammy and her tribe. Since he wasn't a street-fighting tom anymore, it was unlikely that he would infect others. Usually when I stopped by, he would nuzzle my legs, and purr when I scratched around his ears. But whenever he saw me with a carrier or a trap, he gave me a worried look and ran in the other direction.

Then suddenly I didn't see him around anymore. A few months went by without a sighting, and I thought Seymour had left his body, as Gail always puts it. I was sad and I missed him, but all in all, I felt he had lived a rather long and rich life for an alley cat.

One evening I got a call from Carol, a rescuer who lived a few blocks away. "Have you seen Seymour lately?" she asked.

"No," I said, and told her I feared he had died.

"No, he's living over at the parking lot on the other side of the bridge," she said. "I thought it looked like him, and then I looked closer and saw he didn't have any balls, and then I was sure it must be him."

I knew the place, a small lot a few blocks away where the cats got regular meals and were protected by a Cyclone fence. Using a table as a base, Carmen, the caretaker, had constructed a little shelter, and painted "Casa de Gatos" on it. An abandoned car also provided a roof for a few friendly, neutered males that lived in the lot or came by for the occasional meal. Carmen fed them twice daily while looking for real homes for them. I suspected that Seymour, who knew the neighborhood from his cutting-around days, had moved over there because he got frightened by the raccoon that had been reported in the little park. Seymour wasn't as young and strong as he used to be, and he probably knew he was no match for a raccoon. In fact, when I went by to see him at his new lot, he looked as if he had lost weight. His skin hung loose against his frame, and the darkness around his mouth worried me. I thought he ought to come back indoors, and I had finally run into someone who wanted to take a hard-to-place cat. Allison, a friend of Pam's, had a ground floor studio where Seymour could even go outside eventually and sun himself on the patio.

It sounded like a good plan, but when we picked Seymour up, he was listless. He did nothing at Allison's apartment but lie behind her toilet. She started having an unexpectedly strong allergic reaction to him, and after ten days or so we decided to put him back outside temporarily while we looked for a new home. But first we took him to the vet to have him checked out.

Dr. Moscovich looked into his ears, eyes, and mouth, put on special glasses to detect skin problems, poked around his abdomen, and drew some urine from his bladder with a needle. The vet was tisking in a worrisome way. "I'm very sorry, Mr. Seymour," he said. "I'm very sorry."

We knew Seymour wasn't in the greatest shape, but I thought that with a good diet and a place to rest up, he would rebound quickly, like he had before.

Dr. Moscovich, who had never before recommended euthanasia to me, was not at all optimistic. "This is an open-and-shut case," he said. "He's in terrible shape. He's dehydrated and his kidneys are enlarged and hardly working."

So Seymour came home with me. I'm not strictly opposed to euthanasia if I think it will lessen suffering, but I couldn't bring myself to have Seymour put down then and there. Mostly, I didn't feel that I could unilaterally make the decision, since it was Carmen who had been taking care of him most recently.

There was one complication, however. I was in the midst of a sticky, disconcerting situation with my co-op board that had started when a number of cats were seen entering my apartment. One night Carol had asked me if she could use my apartment for an "adoption evening." She had applications from several people who wanted to adopt cats, and she needed a place where people could interact with prospective pets. She had come by with maybe ten cats in four carriers—more animals than I had expected—and she had encountered one of the board members in the courtyard. There had been, I gathered, a bit of a row.

A few weeks later I received a notice saying it was against house rules to harbor multiple animals in the apartments. The note made me uneasy, and I immediately called the building manager, explaining the situation, clarifying that I owned just the one cat, and extending to him an invitation to come and inspect my premises. I told the board president, who lived a couple floors down from me, the same thing. I thought that was the end of it, until a year later when I tried to buy the apartment from Murray at the appraised price.

I was expecting questions about my cat activities at my interview with the board. I imagined rumors had circulated about me. But I thought I could honestly explain that I was only trying to help deal with a neighborhood problem, and that I was not interested in maintaining a menagerie of my own. I hoped I could make them understand that I wasn't a threat. In one of my fantasies, I launched into a spirited defense of the cats and my efforts to manage them, after which I was appointed Animal Control Officer by the board and given broad discretionary powers to deal with the local wildlife.

But I didn't even get an interview—just a certified letter stating that the co-op board had decided to exercise their right of first refusal and buy the apartment directly from Murray, at the price he had offered to me. If he didn't cooperate, his shares would be transferred anyway, and money would be placed in an escrow account for him. In another certified letter, I was notified "as a courtesy" that after the transfer, I would have thirty days to move out.

No one I talked to had heard of such a thing happening. But after consulting with a couple of lawyers, I was surprised to find out how few rights I, as a subtenant, had in the situation. Murray was livid.

"We were going to cancel her sublet anyway," the board president, who had always been very friendly to me in the hallways, told Murray when he called to complain. "We want her out." He explained that years ago the board had problems with a woman who had numerous cats and a neighbor with asthma. The idea of cats, or more probably, cat ladies, seemed to make them nervous. Besides, the board apparently thought that I would be paying too little for the apartment and that the co-op wouldn't get its fair back taxes.

Murray told him that I had just the one cat and that I was helping the co-op manage a potential problem. "What are you going to do about the cats?" Murray asked. "Kill them? Cats have rights, too, you know."

"Oh, no," said the board president. "Oh, no. We're not going to get into *that*."

This was happening at the very height of the most recent real estate boom in Manhattan. Small studios in tenements a few blocks away were renting for $1,600 a month. Co-op prices had doubled in the last year. Even though I felt rather prosperous, the prospect of trying to find an affordable apartment as large as mine in Manhattan was daunting. I knew people who had looked for months and ended up in Queens or Brooklyn. The timing was terrible in other respects as well. I was in the final grueling stages of getting out an important 500-page United Nations report under excruciating deadlines. And Murray and Lois were counting on me for the proceeds from the sale of the apartment, to help pay for their place in the Berkshires, and their closing date had been set.

I hired a new lawyer whose analysis of the by-laws indicated that the co-op had broken a number of procedural rules, which he laid out, point by point, in a sharp letter. Rather than fight me in court, the board agreed to let me stay and buy the place if I paid an additional $10,000 to the co-op in what is called a "flip tax." I also had to sign a statement agreeing never to keep more than two cats at a time in my apartment.

"Maybe it's for the best," said one friend of mine, who, after a year or so of rescuing cats, found himself the proud owner of seven.

It was in the middle of all this that I brought Seymour home from the vet. There was, however, the matter of the standing invitation I'd made to the board president to come up at his convenience. I wanted to show him how orderly and pretty my apartment was, and to let him see that it was just Casey and me.

So having Seymour in the bathroom didn't quite fit into the picture. Besides, during the summer it got steaming hot in there. I kept Seymour for a few days while calling and e-mailing everyone I could think of who might have a place for him. When I found a Pennsylvania cat sanctuary that would give him a comfortable place to die on his own terms, I made arrangements to get him there the following weekend. But in the meantime, it seemed that he might as well stay at Lois's for a just few days until I could transport him, so as not to spoil my chances with the co-op president. It all seemed pretty reasonable, until I goofed up.

The cushion covers looked good when they came back from the cleaners. The special enzymatic cleaning solution had taken the smell out of the foam. And a day or two after Lois, Murray, and Wily got back from the Berkshires, I confessed.

Lois hadn't noticed anything. Her main concern seemed to be whether Seymour could possibly have left germs for Wily, who had never had her booster shots.

Carmen didn't want Seymour to go to Pennsylvania. For a $75 monthly donation, she was able to reserve a spot for him at the Furry Love Kitten Kat Farm, a Manhattan loft space where a veterinary technician cared for and, if necessary, medicated seventy cats or so. One day I called to see if I could visit. A voice on the answering machine responded: "All of the kitty cats are busy with their shenanigans and can't come to the phone right now. But if you leave your message, one of their trusted human servants will get back to you."

Eventually I got in touch with Siobhan, the cats' human servant, and arranged for a visit to the "farm," which turned out to be just a few blocks away, on the top floor of a funky East Village building whose tenants were trying to buy it and bring it up to code. Siobhan, a brawny, tattooed guy with a shaved head, in combat boots and fatigues, met me downstairs. Some of the steps leading up to the fifth floor were mere planks that popped up if you stepped in the wrong spot.

At the landing, Siobhan told me, "We've got to enter together, really quickly, so no one gets out," and we stepped together through the door. The cats were hungry and quickly congregated around a few pounds of raw ground beef that he plunked down.

The large loft, loosely divided into three areas, was mostly unfurnished except for items that might engage, humor, or otherwise serve cats. A two-story row of open cat carriers—Siobhan called them the "Kitty Condos"—lining one wall was feral territory. On the opposite wall, cats were perched on several ladders of varying heights. High catwalks along the walls and a screened-in rooftop garden were part of Siobhan's long-range plans for the "farm."

The most popular spot was a bed at the far end of the loft where a couple dozen very friendly cats lazed among a pile of stuffed animals. A few feet from the bed was an alcove separated from the larger room by a screen door made of chicken wire, the upscale quarters of a few well-behaved "fat cats" and Siobhan's musical equipment. As I watched a pair of kittens scale a heavy curtain hanging from one wall, Siobhan said, "Everything's set up for them."

The place was essentially a home of last resort for cats like Seymour that had nowhere else to go. Many of the cats had FIV or other medical problems. Some were feral, taken off the street when they got old or sick. Siobhan knew the names, histories, or medical problems and personality traits of each cat.

"This one seems very adoptable," I said, petting a gorgeous Norwegian forest cat.

"Her human went homeless," said Siobhan. "But she doesn't want to give up the cat."

Several of the cats, like the extremely personable Lawrence, who was quite attractive in spite of one flattened ear, seemed immune to the charms of litter boxes. As Siobhan and I were speaking, Lawrence casually raised a leg and peed on the wall.

"You can't make a cat stop doing that," said Siobhan, who seemed quite at ease with the strong smell in the place. "That's his way of communicating. It would be like telling you not to write a letter."

One of the older cats stayed in a large chicken wire cage wall in the far room with his good buddy. "He has a paralyzed bladder," Siobhan told me as he lifted the cat from a shelf in the cage, held him over a large stainless steel sink, and squeezed a substantial volume of urine out of him.

"He hates this," Siobhan said.

"Isn't it kind of a relief? Doesn't it make him feel more comfortable?"

"He's so embarrassed by it," Siobhan said, as he tenderly brushed the large white and black kitty. "Sometimes he stands in the litter box and tries to go, but he can't. He's just like a human, but in this furry body. In some ways, he's better than a human."

But where was Seymour? Siobhan directed me to a large neutered tabby on the bed, but it wasn't Seymour. We figured out that Seymour's identity had gotten mixed up with that of another tabby at the vet's office. Siobhan had called Seymour "Grampa," and Grampa had gotten sicker and died.

But Seymour had received royal treatment during his last days, Siobhan assured me. He was given access to the sunny room with the Fat Cats, got fluids each day under his skin and was showered with affection. When Siobhan knew the end was very near, and that Seymour was suffering, he took him to the vet to be euthanized.

"How did they know you rescue cats?" asked one of the women from City Critters when I explained my apartment problem. "Don't you always cover the traps?"

Now I do. Now I follow Vera's lead and put the traps inside laundry bags so as not to arouse suspicion. But initially it didn't occur to me that I was doing anything wrong or had anything to hide. I was naive. It was, after all, only a few hundred years ago that women who were kind to cats were branded as witches, and something of that attitude persists.

I also came to comprehend the seamy, subversive element that surrounds trafficking in live animals, particularly in cats. That it makes people nervous is understandable. Cat rescuing does seem to attract, or create, its share of eccentrics. And dealing with live creatures—especially wild animals—is a huge responsibility, one that, in New York anyway, is pretty much self-regulated. (There are some laws on the subject, but they tend not to be enforced.) As a rescuer, one feels one is working from the highest of motives—but who can be sure about those other people with traps?

Rumors fly among animal lovers. Before I became acquainted with Vera, one of the feeders warned me about the woman from Berlin who trapped cats and sold them to laboratories. They had seen Vera take cats away, they saw that the cats didn't come back, and they thought they knew the score. When I got to know Vera, I realized how ridiculous the rumor was. Even then it seemed to me that breeding cats would be an easier way for laboratories to get their victims than trapping them. But initially the rumor had given me pause.

Simply finding rescue resources can be something of a clandestine activity. Once when I was seeking out someone I thought might be able to foster Seymour, I was directed to a small occult bookstore. When I didn't see any cats, I thought I was in the wrong place. But then I was directed to a door in the very back of the store, which opened up onto another narrow galley space, this one smelling as heavily of cats as the first did of incense. Half a dozen cats were curled up or sauntering about. A slender, dark-haired woman was sitting at a small table with a deck of cards. "Are you here for a reading?" she asked.

Phone numbers for rescuers are not widely advertised because volunteers are often inundated by requests for help. In fact, people who are trying to find homes for cats are cautioned about ads that seem to make finding a home—especially for a feral cat—appear to be easy. These ads may be covers for people who are looking for bait for pit bulls, or who have another sinister agenda. There simply are not many spots readily available for feral cats—unless you happen to get lucky enough to find space in a sanctuary, and even that usually requires a sizeable donation. Although e-mail has improved things considerably, it's best to have personal contacts. To get help, you sometimes have to prove you can be trusted because many cat rescuers are, in fact, violating their leases by keeping animals in their apartments.

Even within circles of cat lovers, there are strongly held but very different approaches that sometimes lead to feuds. Some people think it's terribly wrong to abort a pregnant female. Others think not aborting the cat simply adds to the tragedy of overpopulation. Some people think it cruel to leave cats out in the city. But after observing and working with feral cats for some years, I am now a strong believer in the trap-neuter-return strategy that has been promulgated by Alley Cat Allies for over a decade, and which has been used widely in England and Denmark for dozens of years.

Alley Cat Allies was founded in 1990 by Becky Robinson and Louise Holton. They had come across a colony of feral cats in their Washington, D.C., neighborhood, but couldn't find local agencies willing to help them deal with the cats humanely. They wanted to follow the trap-neuter-return method that was practiced widely in England, but couldn't find anyone willing to help with traps or advice. So the two women essentially started a movement in this country. For more than a decade the group has served as a gold mine of information and advice for others navigating the trap-neuter-return approach to feral cats. During that time it has provided assistance to some sixty thousand care-takers. In the last couple of years their focus has shifted from assisting individuals to influencing public policy.

Simply eradicating populations of feral cats just doesn't work over the long term, according to Alley Cat Allies. Many studies back this up. Cats are simply too successful at breeding and exploiting available ecological niches. Removing cats creates what researcher Roger Tabor calls the vacuum effect: As long as there are food and shelter opportunities in an area, other cats will quickly move in and repopulate it. Managed colonies, on the other hand, tend to protect their space and prevent an influx of new cats. At the same time, the neutering of the animals cuts down on the behaviors that people find objectionable: the cat-erwauling, the spraying, and the fighting. And it halts endless cycles of suffering and population spikes. Everything that Alley Cat Allies preached corresponded to what had I observed during the few years that I looked after Tammy and her tribe. ❖

Chapter 11

Tammy's Tribe

The current public attitude—or paradigm—about feral cats is that they are a public nuisance and health hazard, an animal not to be tolerated in our environment. The new paradigm that is being put forward by ACA and feral cat caretakers—one that has been embraced in many European countries for decades—is that cats are as welcome a part of urban wildlife as squirrels, raccoons, and birds.

—Alley Cat Action

"How many are out there?" a man called one morning when I was leaving food for Tammy's little gang.

"Five," I said. "All the females are spayed."

"That's good," he said. "They're nice-looking cats."

They were, indeed. Many people seemed to derive pleasure from what I'd come to think of as "my cats": I often saw passersby watching them at the feeding station, and one young couple told me they were an endless source of delight for their two-year-old, who watched them from their second floor window. I was quite proud of my beauties, my little pride of wild cats, my healthy managed colony. Often I wouldn't see one of the cats for a few days, and I'd start to worry. But this morning they were all out in the sun, all five present and accounted for. I was proud of beautiful Gemini, with his sumptuous, ebony coat and plumed tail, and Piper, his slightly smaller and less furry twin. I was proud of Callie's independent spirit and her ability to catch rodents near the compactor. I loved watching the antics of Scrappy, a gray youngster with a white bib. Most of all, I was proud that I'd seen the end of reproducing days for sinuous, street-savvy Tammy, the alpha female of the block. With Tammy's tubes finally tied, I could devote less of my time to the constant work of catching her kittens and figuring out what to do with them, and I could think about working on some other tribes nearby.

I had first started keeping an eye on Tammy a couple of years earlier when she was still keeping company with Seymour and Nicholas. I knew that if the population got out of hand, I'd be sorry, and I'd ultimately have a larger problem—or, more aptly, another litter of smaller problems—to contend with. I couldn't bear the thought of another roundup right on my block, under my watch. At that time I was out of town frequently and couldn't keep daily tabs on Tammy, but from what I observed, I wasn't even certain she was fertile. She was so long and lean that she rarely looked pregnant—and I never saw kittens about. It took me several months to figure out that although Tammy was able to maneuver up and down the sixteen-foot basement wall—I think she had a complicated route that included tip-toeing along the water pipes—her kittens probably never made it up to ground level, where the solid food was. Most likely they died down in the basement.

But one, Miles, must have had unusual pluck.

One evening around dusk as I watched Tammy, Nicholas, and Seymour lick themselves clean after eating, I got the distinct impression they were nervous. I wasn't even sure what tipped me off—perhaps ears perking, bodies stiffening, eyes shifting. Then I noticed a couple of furtive glances toward the darkness at the far end of the park. I looked in that direction, too, but couldn't make out anything in the half-light. The next evening, though, I spied movement in the shadows. When I backed off a few feet and hid behind a brick pillar, a tabby baby trotted right over to eat. Or at least he tried to. I was irked that the adults, even the usually sweet Seymour, wouldn't give the little guy a break. Every time the youngster tried to poke his head down to the plate, Tammy, his own mother, batted him back, while Nicholas and Seymour held their ground at the food.

The kitten, Miles, was a funny-looking, scrawny creature with droopy eyes in a head that seemed small compared to his surprisingly round belly. When I returned with a trap, he walked right in for the tuna and stayed quite calm when it closed on him. The next day at the vet's, an exam revealed that his enlarged belly was swollen from parasites, his protective inner eyelid was partially closed due to dehydration, and he was being devoured by fleas.

Miles was the first kitten I subjected to a flea bath. Some kittens don't seem to mind bathing and relax once they are submerged in the warm water. But Miles entered the bucket resisting with the surprising force that a one-and-a-half-pound feline can muster when it thinks it's fighting for its life. His four legs were rigid and splayed, his claws extended, his pupils dilated, his meows frantic. His fear, so palpable, reminded me of something Albert Schweitzer once wrote about the basic primal emotions catching all of us in much the same way.

> Just as in my own will-to-live there is a yearning for more life, and for that mysterious exaltation of the will which is called pleasure, and terror in face of annihilation and that injury to the will-to-live which is called pain; so the same obtains in all around me, equally whether it can express itself to my comprehension or whether it remains unvoiced.

The brilliant observer of nature Charles Darwin also noted more than a century ago that the "difference in mind between man and the higher animals, great as it is, is certainly one of degree rather than of kind." In this era, scientists find more and more evidence that activities which once seemed uniquely human—dreaming, painting, music appreciation, language, tool-making, self-consciousness, prevarication—are shared by other mammals. The more I have worked with cats, the more impressed I am with their, for want of a better word, humanity—their intelligence, perception, sociability, and soulfulness.

Miles had all those winning qualities, and he was quickly situated in a new home. After his appearance, I kept a sharper eye on Tammy's behavior and looked more closely for any discernible changes in girth. But Lulu announced her presence before I realized that Tammy had yet another almost-grown litter stashed in the boiler room.

One morning while working at home, I heard a series of short urgent meows from somewhere outside my building. As best I could tell, they came from seven stories below my bedroom window, from a spot on the opposite side of the building and half a block away from the feeding station. The cries seemed to emanate from a pile of wood scrap and scaffolding in a corner of the cement niche that was visible from my bedroom window. While the volume suggested a female in heat, the cries sounded too staccato for that. What I was sure of, though, was that someone desperately wanted to be heard.

The meowing occurred intermittently for a couple of cold, rainy days. Carol came by, and we poked around the scrap pile. We didn't see or hear anything. I left some cat food out, just in case. Carol said the noise was probably a kitten in distress. I disagreed. I couldn't believe that a kitten could survive that long on its own, let alone project so forcefully and maintain the volume for so long. I would have expected the cries to trail off, like a battery-operated radio running out of juice.

The next day the meowing started again, as loud as before. This time, though, when I went down to investigate, the maintenance man told me a kitten had been seen by the scrap pile.

I set up a trap and waited. It didn't take long before a kitten came sniffing around. Although she'd been calling for help for more than two days, she showed impressive impulse control. She did not just dart in for a meal. She surveyed the trap, circled around it, then went back under cover. She resisted the tuna fish while I waited and walked around the block a few times. Impatient, I went back to my apartment, but, with a pair of opera glasses, I kept an eye on the trap from my bedroom window. Finally, a couple of hours after I placed the trap, the kitten, resistance no doubt worn down by hunger, walked in and the door snapped shut. I ran down, covered the trap, and brought her into my bathroom.

Like her mother, Lulu was a short-haired, Abyssinian-looking tortoiseshell, and like Tammy, she was one tough cat. She had somehow wandered away from the group and, lost, meandered under the building and down a tunnel or pipe before finding her way out—but on the far side of the building, away from the feeding station and the rest of her gang. Perhaps a door had been closed, blocking her way back. But with both the building and the courtyard separating her from Lulu, Tammy couldn't have heard her daughter's sharp cries for help.

Like most of my freshly trapped cats and kittens, this little tortoiseshell hid in the corners of my bathroom for a couple of days, sometimes burrowing between a towel and the wall, so that just a quirk of tail was showing. She couldn't have been

Photo courtesy of Gail Karlsson

much more than six weeks old. Following recommendations for feral kittens, I left her alone for a day while quietly providing food and water. Eager as I was to hold her, I was scared of this fiercely wild thing, even though, by my reckoning, she must have been close to death from hunger and exposure, and could fit, quite literally, in the palm of my hand. Every time I got close, Lulu would lash out explosively, hissing and baring her teeth, giving the word *spitfire* vivid new meaning. An agile friend finally managed to grab hold of her by the nape of the neck. Because that hold emulates a mother's grip, it makes kittens go limp and become relatively helpless. Once swathed in a towel, Lulu calmed down enough so that I could pet her, but she was still ferocious the next day. When I tried to touch her again, a sharp incisor punched neatly through my fingernail and punctured my skin.

I don't know who sired that litter, but I've heard that disposition is inherited through the father, so he must have been fierce as well. When I picked up Lulu's two littermates, they were the most nasty and aggressive kittens I had ever encountered. For months they were in a cage at Vera's, hissing and lashing out at anyone who came too close. I'm still sorry I didn't insist on putting them back in the park. Carol thought she could tame them and adopt them out, but for more than a year they remained essentially incarcerated in her bathroom. Many rescuers think they are doing wild cats a favor by keeping them indoors, no matter what the circumstances. I think these cats are better off roaming free. In any case, I was concerned that Carol, with carriers of kittens piling up in her bathroom, was becoming a collector.

More of Tammy's kittens started showing up after I spoke to the new building supervisor about making a cat-sized opening in a well-positioned vent that would allow them easy access to the basement. It turned out he liked having a few cats to keep the rodent population down. Once the route from the basement to the park was open, it became clear that Tammy was doing her Darwinian best to repopulate the area with her own genes. In less than a year, Vera and I picked up fourteen of Tammy's kittens from three separate litters. Two sets of kittens showed up during the period my apartment was in jeopardy and I was afraid to be seen with traps, so Vera would often come over and do the actual trapping. When I counted back on the five years I had known Tammy, adding in previous litters that the other feeders had told me about, I calculated she must have given birth to at least seventy kittens.

Two of the fourteen kittens that we trapped died from a combination of diarrhea and fleas. Diarrhea can kill a tiny kitten overnight, and fleas, which are especially attracted to sick cats, suck the blood right out of them. By the time I got little Winken (one of the two that didn't make it) to the Animal Medical Center, she was so anemic she could barely lift her head. Her gums, lacking in red blood cells, were the color of ivory. As I held the almost motionless kitten, I felt her heart beat frantically against her matchstick ribs, trying hard to transport oxygen without enough hemoglobin. During the night after a transfusion she died, alone in a stainless steel cage.

A couple of Tammy's kittens were trapped at four or five months, beyond the age when they were readily tamable, and those I neutered and returned. With this approach, the tribe leveled off at seven, stabilizing just as Alley Cat Allies predicted it would. Occasionally I'd see other cats feeding at the regular station, cats I recognized from a block or two over. I noticed them mainly late at night, and from their skulking demeanor, it seemed like they knew they were infringing on someone else's territory. As far as I could tell, Tammy and her gang got to eat first, and if there were leftovers, as there often were, other cats could partake.

Tammy herself had eluded my traps for years. She evidently knew exactly what they were for, and she was not about to trade her freedom for a chunk of sardines. Richard finally managed to snag her, using an ingenious trap of chicken wire and wood he'd designed and built. He could lower it down over cats that were too savvy to enter a suspicious wire contraption, and then slide a plywood bottom underneath and latch it. By the time Richard trapped her, Tammy was clearly pregnant with yet another litter, and was probably so hungry that she was less cautious then usual. When I dropped her off with the vet that Tuesday evening, he told me he wouldn't get to her until Thursday. "Well, okay," I said, "But I hope she makes it—she's pretty far along."

She didn't make it. The night before she was to be spayed, she gave birth to five babies. By morning they were squealing for food, but Tammy was too upset to nurse them. The vet's assistant told me if she didn't start mothering by the next day, they'd begin bottle-feeding the kittens. In the meantime, to afford Tammy some privacy, they put a cardboard box in her cage and covered the barred door with a blanket. "Being watched is like torture to a feral cat," Anitra Frazier, a well-known cat expert, had told me when I called her for advice.

The next day, just as the vet was getting bottles and formula together, Tammy relented. Perhaps she could no longer ignore the plaintive squealing or perhaps the flower essence remedy they put on her food kicked in. Whatever the reason for Tammy's change of heart, she started nursing and mothering. If she hadn't, I'm not sure what I would have done. I couldn't imagine finding someone with the time to bottle-feed five youngsters several times a day. We'd also have had to find another cat, possibly even a neutered male, who would be willing to undertake part of their care: to lick them clean and teach them cat ways.

After two weeks we transported Tammy and her brood to a neighbor of Pam's, who had volunteered to foster the family for a month or so. Richard had borrowed a large cattery with shelves for Tammy to hop up on when she needed to get away from the demands of her children, and she raised a lovely kindle of kittens. That's a now-archaic term for a litter of kittens, from the Middle English word *kindler*, "to give birth." When grown up, they would once have been called a *clowder* of cats, probably derived from the word *clutter*. Murray pointed out that *kindle* sounded a lot like kindling, and we didn't like the implications of that at all. Watching Tammy's brood grow, week by week from unsteady, half-blind, mewing balls of fur into pouncing, climbing, slightly clumsy, and rambunctious playmates, other terms came to mind: a chaos of kittens, a mischief of kittens, a commotion of kittens, an amusement of kittens. Fortunately they were adopted quickly, two to the woman who had lovingly cared for them, two to her mother, and one to someone else in the building. I was thankful that Tammy's pregnancy had ended up so well, redeeming what had seemed at first to be a complication of kittens, or worse, a catastrophe of them.

With their intense communicativeness, affection, and playful ease around people, Tammy's kittens stood in sharp contrast to their mom. During the day, Tammy stayed put in the back corner of the cage, eyes watchful but grim. She'd swipe at anyone who came too close and once nipped her caretaker. "She looks depressed, doesn't she?" I asked Pam one day when we went to visit.

"She looks pissed," said Pam. And she did. Konrad Lorenz has said that no animal communicates more through its facial expressions than the cat. Its eyes can harden into a glare or soften into a caress. Its pupils dilate or constrict, its whiskers flatten or come forward, its ears can perk right up or lie back against its head. Though Tammy was being a good mommy to her kittens, when she looked at us, her face seemed full of contempt.

After her kittens were eight weeks old and we'd seen to her spaying, I took Tammy back to the park to release her. Like many other captives on the brink of freedom, she stayed at the back of the carrier for several minutes after I opened the door. Finally I upended the carrier a bit, and she tore straight for the basement vent, ten yards away. Gemini, who had been off in the bushes, watched her dash in, and then he, too, made a run for the hole in the wall. About a minute later, he shot out just as fast. Perhaps he had run out to tell the others, but then again, maybe he and his long-lost mom had had a spat.

"You put her back?" asked the rescuer from whom we had borrowed the cattery. She was obviously disappointed in me.

"Oh, she'll be fine," I said. "She's a wild one." By that time I had come to trust my sense of what is best for cats. And I knew Tammy pretty well. I did not want to be responsible for her living out her life ill at ease in some crowded apartment—not when she had familiar territory and a band of her own waiting for her.

"She's got a safe spot, and she's the queen bee out there," I said. Besides, the members of her tribe had seemed insecure and confused with her away. They didn't hang around at the usual times. They didn't seem to cluster together in the same way. With the matriarch gone, they didn't act like a clan.

I didn't see Tammy for a week after I put her back. But then one night there she was, waiting for dinner and looking great. Back in her own space, with her offspring, she seemed to sparkle. When I opened a tin of food, she came right up, met my eyes, and started eating, not more than a foot from where I stood but on the other side of the iron fence. The others hung back. It seemed pretty clear that even after her confinement among the humans, Tammy was still the undisputed leader of her pack.

I wish I could say things ended so neatly, but I hadn't tied up every single loose end. I hadn't worried much about getting the last trap-shy kitten, Scrappy. For some reason—probably wishful thinking—I had decided Scrappy was a male. But he turned out to be a she, and two litters and much effort later I was wishing I had been more diligent. One female cat, as I well knew, can quickly turn into a population explosion.

A couple of Scrappy's kittens disappeared and the rest I eventually trapped, but not without problems. Timing is critical when it comes to kittens. Too little time with their mothers and they often have health problems. Too much time and they become hard to socialize. I erred on both sides. I managed to trap kittens from the first litter too young, at five or six weeks. They had diarrhea, fleas, goopy eyes, and they failed to thrive. Even though she was overwhelmed with her own cats, Vera was kind enough to provide the constant attention it took—twice-daily eyedrops, parasite medication, Kaopectate and rice water in their food—to nurse them back to health. They remained fierce for a week or so, and it was more than a month before they were healthy and socialized enough for adoption.

With the next litter I procrastinated, and the kittens turned out to be healthy but feisty and untouchable. If kittens have no human contact by the time they are eight weeks old, they become very difficult to socialize. Not having the time to give them the attention they needed, I put two back into the colony after they were neutered, and my accountant and his wife were willing to foster and work with the other two.

Besides Tammy's tribe, other cats sometimes drift into the area. I suspect some were mousers for local establishments who'd either escaped, been turned out, or gotten lost. So even after my entire tribe is spayed, there will clearly be more work to do. Nature doesn't stay in a steady state for long. But one thing has changed dramatically since I first got involved with the courtyard cats years ago: there are now considerable resources available to make the work easier. ❖

— Chapter 12 —

Going to Scale

The ethic of Reverence for Life . . . keeps us watching together for opportunities to bring some sort of help to animals in recompense for the great misery that men inflict upon them, and thus for a moment we escape from the incomprehensible horror of existence.

—*Albert Schweitzer,* Civilization and Ethics

"Trap-neuter-return is a long-term method to control and decrease the number of feral, free-roaming cats," Dr. Margaret Slater, a veterinary epidemiologist from Texas A&M University was telling a crowded roomful of people at the American Society for the Prevention of Cruelty to Animals in March 2001. "Pulling out individual cats and euthanizing them doesn't work because we're dealing with herds. On the other hand, neutered cats will settle down, hold territory to a certain extent, and can live to be twelve to fourteen years old."

The afternoon workshop was the first time one of the large animal organizations in the city had offered a program specifically on feral cats. In a carefully organized slide presentation, Dr. Slater, a trim, articulate woman who appeared to be in her late thirties, discussed various options for dealing with populations of free-roaming cats. Doing nothing means population spikes, considerable suffering, and nuisance complaints. Removing and killing cats is expensive and ineffective over the long term, in addition to being, arguably, a denial of the right of other beings to exist. Removal and relocation is impractical because sanctuaries quickly reach their limits. Most promising is the trap-neuter-return method (often expanded to include testing, vaccinating, and ear-tipping—a way of marking cats that have already been spayed or neutered), whose success was validated by data that Slater presented from half a dozen community programs.

Slater had gotten involved with the issue of feral cats when they began creating something of a crisis in and around Texas A&M's campus in College Station, Texas. Unowned, free-ranging cats often are problematic on college campuses—as well as on military bases—because their transient residents tend toward a higher-than-usual rate of pet abandonment. These left-behind pets swell whatever cat populations already exist. The comprehensive trap-neuter-return program initiated at Texas A&M in 1998 turned the feral cat issue into what the college's Web site called "a unique educational tool for veterinary and wildlife sciences students." Graduate wildlife and epidemiology students observed and trapped cats; fourth-year veterinary students gained experience with surgeries and medical procedures and in handling feral cats; and other campus volunteers served as feeders and caretakers. The school's dairy barns were able to utilize the all-natural rodent management services of the cats without having to deal with feline overpopulation.

The program, which eventually formed the basis for several studies and spawned a similar community-based program in surrounding Brazos County, resulted in the capture of 158 cats, 20 percent of which proved to be adoptable. The program brought the number of kittens born in the second year of the program to zero, and complaints about cats plummeted as well. In addition, the program attracted positive publicity for the school's College of Veterinary Medicine, and it averted the public relations nightmare that institutions face when they start exterminating large numbers of cats.

One of Slater's slides showed a graph plotting ten years' worth of data from Orange County, Florida, where a nonprofit feral cat organization had partnered with the county animal control agency to undertake a large-scale, long-term trap-neuter-return program. Over the decade, nuisance complaints and the number of cats euthanized dropped by 20 percent, adoptions were up, and impoundments down. Community relations were much improved and expenditures were down. Trap-neuter-return programs often end up costing less than the more traditional approach because it is possible to mobilize volunteers when the mission is saving, rather than killing, feral cats.

A few months after the initial ASPCA program on feral cats, a committee of the Association of the Bar of the City of New

York offered a seminar on legal issues pertaining to feral cats. The Bar Association's large auditorium was packed—perhaps two hundred people had ventured out on a Wednesday evening to learn how the legal system views street cats. (The short answer is that feral cats are currently somewhat below their radar screen. Municipalities are often reluctant to get involved with feral cats, both because they pose few public safety problems—unlike packs of feral dogs—and because dealing with them is such a time-consuming process.) Both of these large meetings suggest a kind of sea change with regard to feral cats—to my knowledge, this was first time they had been deemed worthy of serious public discourse. At the Bar Association meeting, the establishment by Art for Animals of a Feral Cat Relief Fund to help caretakers with expenses was also announced.

More positive things started happening. That summer the Humane Society of New York initiated a formal feral cat clinic on Sundays, as a convenience to caretakers with regular jobs. The clinic provided free neutering, rabies shots, treatment for ear mites and fleas, and ear tipping. All that colony caretakers with appointments have to do is bring in feral cats in traps and then pick them up later in the day. Workshops on the basics of trap-neuter-return, as well as a hands-on workshop on how to construct simple Styrofoam cat shelters were offered at the ASPCA. The ASPCA also started working with caretakers to spay and neuter outdoor colonies, using its mobile van/operating theater, and it set up a lending bank of traps for those who needed them.

More individuals began to get involved. One morning as I passed by *my* cats, I was surprised to find a woman who had traveled down from the East Village with traps, tuna fish, and sardines because she had heard about the tribe and wanted to get them under control. Much of this activity was initiated or given impetus by Neighborhood Cats, a group I'd become acquainted with a few months earlier. Neighborhood Cats was the first organization in the city to actively advocate and work toward reducing feral cat populations by neutering individual cats and maintaining them in colonies, an idea that was still contentious among rescuers.

Neighborhood Cats was founded by an interesting and capable threesome with complementary talents and a shared sense of commitment: Bryan Kortis, an attorney and video filmmaker; Shirley Belwood, a prop-master for major films; and Ruth Sharp, a bookstore and a day care center manager, and member of the Secular Franciscan Order with an apostolate centered on animal issues. The three had come to know one another as each was trying independently, without success, to find the resources to deal with a sudden surge in the cat population in an open area between buildings on their Upper West Side block.

"We didn't want to take in fifteen cats each," Bryan said. "But we didn't want to walk away from the situation, either." He started knocking on doors and talking to people on the block, finding out who was interested in the cats. Initially the group followed a traditional rescue model: trapping and vetting the cats, placing them in foster homes, and then trying to adopt them out. But like me, they quickly discovered that feral cats presented major challenges. As the group's Web site notes: "After a brief stint of cats climbing walls in people's bathrooms and not acting like sweet pussycats, we learned the difference between domestic and feral. If we were going to continue our work without filling our apartments with unadoptable cats, like so many other rescuers had done, we had to find another way."

Using guidelines from Alley Cat Allies, the group had gotten several colonies in their neighborhood under control, while carefully documenting each effort. They formed a non-profit corporation, set up a Web site, made a video, and took on a host of other activities aimed both at helping individuals become caretakers and changing the climate of public opinion. The group didn't believe the time was right to attempt to affect city policy on feral cats. They did want to have some model colonies established and documented, so that whenever city policy toward feral cats becomes an issue, Neighborhood Cats can demonstrate that they have a humane and viable solution.

Their measured, open, inclusive, and organized approach compared quite favorably to—well, to tell the truth, there was little comparison—the furtive, ad hoc, crisis-oriented way I had originally gone about things. In my own defense, however, I suspect that the Neighborhood Cats brand of community activism is easier to find support for on the famously progressive Upper West Side than in my neighborhood.

The group's idea is not simply to help street cats but to "go to scale" with the managed-colony approach—to multiply the effect of their efforts by offering support and guidance that others need to get other colonies under control. Neighborhood Cats seemed both effective and grounded in reality. When members get word of a problem colony, they offer help only if the people who reported the cats are willing to shoulder most of the responsibility, including transport, recovery space, and long-term colony maintenance. They organize and present workshops at the ASPCA dealing with the whole gamut of issues associated with feral cats, from public relations to taming feral kittens to health and safety issues to fund-raising. To this latter point, they passed out a model letter they'd devised to gain support for individual projects, and which was sent, using realtors' mailing lists, to everyone on the block near the colony in question:

"Dear Neighbors," one such letter began. "You have probably heard, seen, or been disturbed by the feral cats that have taken residence in the backyards of our block. Through the years this colony has grown steadily and almost out of control. The good news is that finally something humane is being done to control the colony's further growth."

After explaining the trap-neuter-return strategy, the letter suggested several ways people could help: by donating money, by placing small shelters in their backyards, by volunteering, or by helping to find homes for friendly cats or kittens. One such letter netted $1,300, mostly from people living on the ground floors. When dealing with busy New Yorkers, raising money is often easier than finding people who can volunteer time.

On the first Thursday of every month, Neighborhood Cats—along with anyone else who is interested—meets in an Upper West Side coffeehouse to discuss plans for the coming

Photo courtesy of Meredith Weiss

months. At one meeting the group discussed the Feral Cat Relief Fund, which they had been asked to administer; at another meeting they considered the logistics of trapping a colony of cats living in a subterranean railroad tunnel in Riverside Park. For some months after September 11, 2001, at the request of the ASPCA, the group helped to trap nine cats left behind in small stores and restaurants near the site of The World Trade Center. Bryan maintained an active e-mail list, and almost daily he sent out notices about cats needing homes, orphaned kittens needing nursing mothers, free food being distributed to caretakers, workshops being offered, large-scale trapping efforts requesting volunteers, and, at least once, a note from people who were looking for kittens.

One sunny January day I joined Bryan, Ruth, and other members of Neighborhood Cats to work with a colony of perhaps twenty cats—since they were all variations on a theme of black and white, it was hard to get an exact count—living in, around, and under the vast infrastructure of one of the city's large bridges. Because female cats are not usually in estrus during the darkest months of winter, January is an ideal time to do large-scale neutering: one is less likely to catch nursing mothers and inadvertently leave vulnerable kittens behind.

We met in a wedge that was bordered by a tangle of Cyclone fencing, in what seemed to be a construction site under the maze of the curved approaches to the bridge. The cacophony of cars whizzing over and around us must have been hard on the sensitive hearing of the cats, but apparently they'd adapted to the noise. They did have one nice perk, "the city's largest litter box," as Eric, the colony caretaker, described a mountain of sand stashed under the bridge.

The group carefully set seven traps and then left the immediate vicinity to help the cats feel more bold, heading to a nearby vantage point from which they could keep an eye on the traps and any activity around them.

"Where are these cats going after you get them?" I asked.

"The CACC. They've agreed to do a pilot program to see how well this works."

I was amazed that Neighborhood Cats had found a way to work effectively with the city's Center for Animal Care and Control, a long-time target for criticism from most other local animal groups. The Center had agreed to transport the trapped cats to its facility for spaying or neutering and had even built a special recovery space for the cats. "We'll work with anyone who's willing to help advance trap-neuter-return," said Ruth. The Center itself was evaluating whether the trap-neuter-release strategy would be more cost-effective than its long-time policy of responding to complaints about cats by picking up and killing them. (Like many other animal advocates, I resist using the word *euthanize* when the killing is done not, strictly speaking, for the cats' own good but for human convenience.)

By the end of the day four cats had been captured, and the next week, one more. (Ten had been trapped a few months earlier, two of which were adoptable.) These five were neutered and put back to live in the underbelly and shadows of the massive bridge, a bleak urban landscape where, it appeared, not even a blade of grass had managed to take root nor any of the scruffy weed-trees that spring up in the city's vacant lots. A couple of unneutered cats remain, but so far there has been no sign of kittens.

"I really think it's cruel to release cats in New York City," a woman from one of the rescue groups said during a discussion that took place toward the end of the ASPCA seminar on feral cats that Dr. Slater had addressed. Others weighed in with their perspectives on the issue. Many felt that all cats should have a chance for domestication. A few days after the meeting, Bryan Kortis circulated his thoughts on the subject to his e-mail correspondents.

> One recurring question at the ASPCA seminar was: How could people be expected to release cats back into uncertain and dangerous circumstances? I believe this is a crucial question that must be fully faced if managed colonies are to take hold in New York City. Because this is a dense urban area, perhaps the densest in the country, there are unique problems with the environment— buildings being torn down, difficult access, and just, in general, gritty urban conditions. Who would ever want to let a cat go in that? I don't think anyone really wants to. It never feels good to me to let a cat go. When I look at a cat before its release, I always have an urge to protect him or her, to keep maybe one more in my home, spared from the dangers of the streets. I have to overcome this feeling and open the door of the carrier. I feel guilty. I worry about them.
>
> Sometimes they go missing and I don't see them again and I wonder what happened. Every time I do see them, I feel relieved and grateful. So how could I have let them go? Because I want to help solve the whole

problem, not just a piece of it. I want to see the day come when no kittens are born on the street. And that day isn't going to come by rescuing one cat at a time, not when there are several hundred thousand of them. It might come, though, if all the ferals were neutered. As I wrote to one of our members who was wrestling with this issue, the pain of releasing them is part of the price of the solution. I also let them go because I can't do any more for them than that. I can't bring any more cats into my home. I've been through the route of finding a sanctuary, and maybe once in awhile you can squeeze your way in, but really they're full. I have no more people I know who will take a feral cat, and I can't afford to board them or pay for their socialization. But I can trap them, neuter them, put them back, and provide them with food and shelter. So rather than do nothing, I choose to do that. I respect the decision of anyone who does work with each cat trapped until it is placed somewhere safe off the streets. But I also respect those who take the managed colony approach and, in so doing, also improve the situation.

People I meet at the feeding station behind my building never fail to mention how healthy and happy the cats there look. They are all Tammy's progeny, although Tammy herself disappeared about six months after I returned her to her tribe. What could have happened? She had seemed very healthy. She had survived so many years that she had to have been well versed in the dangers of the basement: the compactors, the moving parts, the wells a cat might fall into. And since she, who seemed so smart and streetwise, is gone, I worry from time to time about the others as well. Even though their current situation is quite protected—even deluxe by New York standards—I am concerned that someday someone will close off the access to the basement again or that the cats will be poisoned or run over or wounded by a firecracker thrown by someone cruel.

But in the meantime, I enjoy knowing they are able to avail themselves of the opportunities for food and shelter that this urban landscape provides, maintaining themselves at a higher density than they probably could in more "natural" environments. I put *natural* in quotes because, as Bill McKibben pointed out in his 1989 book *The End of Nature*, there are no truly natural places left, no places untouched by the enormous footprint of human activity. Traces of dangerous man-made chemicals are found in the arctic ice caps, human activity has eroded the atmosphere's protective ozone layer, species are disappearing at a rate not seen since the end of the dinosaur's reign, and we have, in a century, altered the weather systems to which life-forms have adapted over millennia. To be successful, plants and animals must find ways to live in this altered world.

Actually, it is these overwhelming global issues—climate change, ozone depletion, population pressures, loss of biodiversity—that I spend much of my time fretting about and much of my professional life working on. Compared to these complex environmental crises, dealing with feral cats is a refreshingly tractable problem. And in a world where it seems so difficult to make a real difference, it is gratifying to have a small but tangible effect: to save one lonely kitty, to look after one little tribe.

When I see Tammy's tribe frolicking in the sunshine, I know that I have made a little difference—and not just to the cats. On my way to work one recent morning, I dropped off a plate of food at the feeding station and cleared away some of the mess left over from the night before. Scrappy kept her distance at first and then scampered to the dish as I walked away. Just as I was leaving, I heard someone call from the seventh or eighth floor of the next building over. I looked up to see a fragile-looking, white-haired, and, to my mind, housebound woman sitting by the window. She pointed down to Scrappy and waved, and then she blew me a kiss. 🐾

Epilogue

Since the rescue of the courtyard cats, five years ago now, I have participated in the catching, trapping, or placing of perhaps sixty cats and kittens. Simply knowing how to help makes it difficult to ignore a pregnant female or a vulnerable tribe.

The work is easier now that I have a network of support. It is not without rewards: There is an undeniable satisfaction in being able to picture so many cats, who would otherwise be dead or miserable, now happily situated. I think of Mimi and Kaspar lying on pillows in Ted's living room with the sun streaming in from the wide meadow outside. I recall Wily's rough tongue licking the palm of my hand and then the spaces between my fingers. The shiest of the courtyard litter, she has blossomed as an "only child" and will jump up on the couch and squeeze in between Lois and Murray for long petting sessions.

Bandit stays out of sight, when I visit Pam and John, but they show pictures of him embracing his buddy Noodle, and tell me of his confusion over the human baby who now shares their lives.

Mr. Nicholas is so eager for attention that he follows his new owner around like a dog. Seymour is gone but not forgotten—Siobhan videotaped the rather elaborate funeral he arranged for him. And the stain Seymour left on Lois's couch, which I thought I had eradicated, has become increasingly visible with time.

Tammy came back—or did she? Soon after she seemingly disappeared, another tortoise shell showed up with exactly the same markings—down to the three white dots under the nose. Although the new cat's body is much more filled out than Tammy's, the vet said that could be the result of her spaying. In any case, this tortoise shell presides over the little tribe just like Tammy did.

Tammy's wild progeny are all hearty and seem very much at ease in the little park next door. I have been trying, without success, to get Scrappy, the last unspayed female of the bunch, but she so far has eluded the traps. I'm watching her carefully now, because I know she has another litter tucked away.

And my Casey, at nineteen, seems to be on the tail end of her ninth life. I give her daily injections of fluids, as well as a number of other medications and nutritional supplements. When the man I'm going to marry came into my life about six months ago, she abandoned my bed and bedroom, and took to the couch, ignoring all my efforts to coax her back. I think it's

more a matter of propriety than anger, though. Just last week, she climbed into Gerald's lap, an unprecedented show of affection, or at least acceptance, for someone other than me.

A few times, when her breathing has been especially labored and her food hasn't stayed down, I've considered helping to ease her out of her body. But each time the idea became a plan, she would suddenly show signs of life—an interest in exploring the hallway, for instance, or a renewed zest for food. She probably can't stand the idea of some new young foundlings taking her place. She needn't worry. Several cats are waiting in the wings for a spot to open up in my apartment. But Casey's place in my heart is sewn up. 🐾

Gerald Tallon

About the Author

After earning a degree in anthropology from Northwestern University, Janet Jensen worked for several years as a journalist in northern Idaho before relocating to New York City. She abandoned a successful career in advertising to pursue graduate work in environmental studies, and is now a freelance writer and editor on environment and development issues for the United Nations. She lives in Manhattan's Lower East Side.